The Big Book of Bible Games

These Bible Learning Games can be some of the most valuable—
and enjoyable—times in your program.
Each game can be played in approximately 20-25 minutes.
The games provide an exciting way to help your students:
- review Bible memory verses
- recall Bible stories and truths already learned
- apply Bible truths to daily living.

Before beginning the games, discuss with your class the purpose of the games and
what attitudes will help all participants to have an enjoyable time.

Gospel Light

How to make clean copies from this book.

You may make copies of portions of this book with a clean conscience if:

✦ you (or someone in your organization) are the original purchaser.

✦ you are using the copies you make for a noncommercial purpose (such as teaching or promoting a ministry) within your church or organization.

✦ you follow the instructions provided in this book.

However, it is illegal for you to make copies if:

✦ you are using the material to promote, advertise or sell a product or service other than for ministry fund-raising.

✦ you are using the material in or on a product for sale.

✦ you or your organization are **not** the original purchaser of this book.

By following these guidelines you help us keep our products affordable. Thank you.

Gospel Light

William T. Greig, Publisher
Dr. Elmer L. Towns, Senior Consulting Publisher
Billie Baptiste, Publisher, Research, Planning and Development
Christy Weir, Senior Editor
Dr. Gary S. Greig; Wesley Haystead, M.S.Ed., Senior Consulting Editors
Bayard Taylor, M.Div., Editor, Theological and Biblical Issues
Linda Mattia, Associate Technical Editor
Linda Bossoletti, Editorial Coordinator

Contents

Contents

JUNIOR GAMES Fifth & Sixth Grade

Bible Story Review

Bible Memory Verse Review

Life Application

Primary Games

High-Rise Window Wash-off

Materials Checklist

- ☐ chalk and chalkboard, or butcher paper and felt pen
- ☐ paper
- ☐ pencil

Preparation

On sheet of paper, write several sentence clues for each of the characters in the session's Bible story—at least one sentence for every two students. Sentences can describe things a character did or quote what a character said. (Examples: She and her family moved to a new land. [Naomi.] She said, "Your people will be my people. Your God will be my God." [Ruth.]) On chalkboard or butcher paper draw two high-rise buildings with lots of windows (sketch a).

How to Use

Divide class into two teams. Review the characters that were in the session's Bible story. Then have teams line up on opposite sides of chalkboard or butcher paper. Teacher stands in the middle and reads the first character clue. Team One guesses which character is being described. If the correct name is guessed, the first player gets to "wash" one window on his team's high-rise by coloring it in with chalk or felt pen (sketch b). Continue game by reading a clue for Team Two. If either team guesses incorrectly, the other team gets a chance to guess. The team with the most windows washed wins. If time allows, play game a second time using the same clues.

Primary/Bible Story Review

Grapes on the Vine Game

Materials Checklist

- [ ] index cards
- [ ] felt pen
- [ ] heavy green yarn

Preparation

Choose a Bible story children have studied. On each index card, letter a true or false statement about an event in the Bible story. Make at least one card for each child in the group.

Examples: True or False?

Jesus was born in a house.(F)

Jesus' mother was Mary.(T)

God is Jesus' true Father.(T)

When Jesus grew up, He became a doctor.(F)

Jesus taught people about God's love.(T)

Jesus made sick and crippled people well again.(T)

Everybody liked Jesus.(F)

Jesus died on a cross.(T)

Jesus came back to life in 10 days.(F)

How to Use

Teacher holds length of yarn and says, **Let's pretend this yarn is a grapevine. When you answer a question about our Bible story correctly, you can be a grape on this grapevine.**

Children sit in a circle on the floor. Place index cards facedown in center of circle. The teacher walks around outside of circle and taps a child on the head saying, **Won't you come and join our line? Hop on board this great, green vine!** Child picks card from stack, reads statement and answers "true" or "false." If child answers incorrectly, he or she returns to place in circle. If child answers correctly, he or she holds on to the yarn and becomes a grape on the vine. The teacher continues to circle around the room with child. The newest grape on the vine taps a child on the head and all grapes recite, **Won't you come and join our line? Hop on board this great, green vine.** Continue game until all children have had an opportunity to participate and are holding on to the vine.

Campfire Roast

Materials Checklist

- [ ] children's music cassette and cassette player
- [ ] paper
- [ ] pencil
- [ ] cast-iron skillet or large pot
- [ ] stick
- [ ] firewood
- [ ] marshmallows—one for each child plus several extras

Preparation

Prepare a list of questions relating to the life application of the Bible story. (E.g., What is one way to grow in wisdom? What is one thing we can do to choose friends carefully? What type of person makes a good friend? What could happen if you don't plan carefully? What is one way to be kind to a friend? mom? brother? etc.) Arrange firewood to form a "campfire." Place one marshmallow on the end of a stick. Place the remaining marshmallows in the skillet and place skillet on top of campfire.

Procedure

Children sit in a circle around the campfire. As cassette is played, children pass stick with marshmallow around the circle. The child holding the stick when the music stops must answer a question asked by the teacher. If the child answers correctly, he or she may take and eat a marshmallow from the skillet. Continue playing until each child has gotten a marshmallow.

River Tug-of-War

Materials Checklist

- [ ] one large inner tube
- [ ] masking tape
- [ ] 8-10 index cards

Preparation

On each index card, letter a simple question about the session's Bible story. Spread cards facedown on a table. Using masking tape, make two parallel lines on the floor approximately 8 feet (2.4 m) apart (sketch a). The space between the lines becomes the "river." Place the inner tube in the river (sketch a).

Procedure

Divide the class into two teams. Teams line up on opposite sides of river. Choose tallest person from each team to begin the game. These two players stand back-to-back inside the inner tube (sketch b). At a given signal, the two players inside the inner tube try to pull each other to their team's side of the river. The winner walks to the question table, chooses a card and reads the question to his or her team. If the team answers correctly, the player from the opposite team must join the winning team. If they answer incorrectly, the player may go back to his or her original team. Continue game until all cards have been used. Team with the most players at the end of the game is the winner.

a.

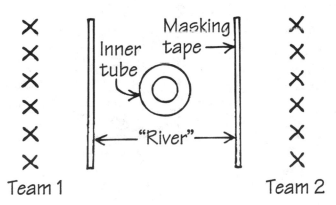

b.

Who's in the Tent?

Materials Checklist

- ☐ Bible
- ☐ small pup tent
- ☐ 15-18 large index cards
- ☐ felt pen
- ☐ chalkboard and chalk or poster board

Preparation

Set up the tent at the front of the room. On each index card letter two or three "I am" statements describing a particular character from the Bible story (see sketch). Each succeeding question should reveal more about the character. Make cards for as many Bible story characters as possible. Letter the answer at the bottom of the card.

Procedure

Divide class into two teams. A volunteer from Team One chooses a card and sits in the tent. Player reads first "I am" statement aloud and chooses a teammate to guess the answer. (Teacher may assist beginning readers.) If the answer is correct, Team One receives three points. If answer is incorrect, second statement is read and another team member is chosen to guess the answer. A correct answer earns two points for Team One. If guess is incorrect the third statement is read. A correct answer now earns Team One one point. If guess is incorrect, a volunteer from Team Two may guess answer. If guess is correct, Team Two earns one point. Record points on chalkboard. Repeat procedure, having volunteer from Team Two choose a question card and sit in the tent. Play continues until all cards have been used. Team with the most points wins.

> 1. I am a disciple. Who am I?
> 2. I love money. Who am I?
> 3. I kissed Jesus. Who am I?
>
> (Judas)

Primary/Bible Story Review

Pony Express

Materials Checklist

- ☐ Bible
- ☐ envelopes
- ☐ index cards
- ☐ felt pen
- ☐ blindfold
- ☐ a chair for each child

Preparation

On each index card, letter a question about the session's Bible story—one for each child (see sketch). Place each card in a separate envelope. Place chairs in two rows facing each other.

Procedure

Children sit in chairs. Each child is given an envelope. Teacher or helper is blindfolded and stands between the two rows of chairs. Teacher calls the name of one child in row A and directs that child to deliver his or her letter to a child in row B. The child attempts to deliver the letter without being tagged by the blindfolded teacher. If the child is tagged, he or she must open the letter and try to answer the question. If the letter is delivered successfully, the recipient reads the question and any volunteer may answer the question. Continue game until all letters have been delivered and all questions answered.

| What was Paul like before he met Jesus? | What did Paul see on the road to Damascus? | Who helped Paul? |

Musical Hats

Materials Checklist

- [ ] children's music cassette and cassette player
- [ ] slips of paper
- [ ] felt pens
- [ ] straight pins
- [ ] masking tape
- [ ] chairs
- [ ] one hat for each child

Preparation

On each slip of paper, letter the name of a character or group from the Bible story. (You can use the names twice if necessary.) Pin one name to each hat (see sketch).

Procedure

Children sit on chairs in a circle. Teacher plays music on cassette as children pass hats around the circle. When the music stops, children put on the hats they are holding. Then teacher closes his or her eyes, spins around in the center of the circle, then stops, pointing at a player. That player must tell the group one fact about the character whose name is on his or her hat. Continue playing until all children have had a turn. Children may not repeat facts stated earlier in the game.

Pass the Mike

Materials Checklist
☐ cassette recorder
☐ blank cassette tape
☐ microphone
☐ timer

Preparation
None.

Procedure
Children take turns telling portions of the Bible story by speaking into the microphone. When first child begins story, set the timer for 30 seconds. When the timer rings, the child must pass the microphone to the next child. When each child has had a turn and the story has been told, listen to the recording.

Hot Potato

Materials Checklist

☐ children's music cassette and cassette player

☐ felt pen

☐ potato

For each child—

☐ index card

Preparation

On each index card, letter a question about the session's Bible story, such as: Who is God's Son? Who told the people to get ready for God's Son? Where did John baptize Jesus?

Procedure

Instruct children to sit in a circle on the floor. While music from cassette is played, children pass a potato around the circle. When the music stops, the child holding the potato answers a question from the index cards. Children may choose a card and read the question aloud or have the teacher read it. If the child does not know the answer he or she may choose a friend to answer the question. Continue game until all children have had an opportunity to participate.

Who is God's Son?

Where did John baptize Jesus?

Who told the people to get ready for God's Son?

Potato Pass

Materials Checklist

- [ ] potato
- [ ] cassette of lively children's music
- [ ] cassette player
- [ ] large paper bag
- [ ] pictures and flannelgraph figures from Bible stories
- [ ] chairs

Preparation

Place chairs in a circle. Place pictures and figures in paper bag.

Procedure

Children sit on chairs in a circle. Teacher plays music on cassette while children pass a potato around the circle. When the music stops, the child holding the potato takes a picture or flannelgraph figure out of the paper bag and tells something about it. *Optional:* You may want to help the child by asking a review question. For example: **Who is this person? Where did he go? Why did he decide to go back home? How do you think he felt when he saw his father?**

Setting the Scene

Materials Checklist

- ☐ large paper bag
- ☐ large index cards
- ☐ hole punch
- ☐ string
- ☐ felt pens
- ☐ highlighter pen

Preparation

Letter the name of a character from the lesson's Bible story on each card. Also letter "man," "woman," "boy," "girl" as needed for crowd scenes until there is a card for each child in your class. Punch two holes in each card and tie on string so children can wear cards. Place all completed cards in paper bag. Use highlighter pen to divide Bible story in Teacher's Book into workable scenes. (Example: Jesus Visits Mary and Martha; Lazarus Becomes Sick and Dies; A Message Is Sent to Jesus; Jesus Comes to Help; Lazarus Is Alive Again.)

Procedure

Let each child draw a card from the paper bag and put it on. Children act out Bible story, playing the parts designated by their cards. Use subtitles to divide story into workable scenes. Announce each scene and the characters that will be needed. Prompt children if necessary by asking questions such as "What do you think Jesus was saying to Mary and the disciples?" "How did the people feel when Lazarus died?" "How can you show sadness?" Indicate when each scene is over. When play is completed, interview characters by asking questions such as "Mary, how did you feel when Jesus came to your house to visit?" "Martha, how did you feel when you were cooking and Mary was doing nothing to help?"

Clothespin Characters

Materials Checklist

- [ ] several clothespins for each child
- [ ] wideneck jar
- [ ] tagboard
- [ ] felt pen
- [ ] small chair
- [ ] length of clothesline for rope
- [ ] tacks

Preparation

Cut tagboard into 4-6 large pennant shapes. Letter the names of the main characters from the Bible story (or several stories) on pennants—one name on each pennant as in sketch. Attach ends of clothesline to bulletin board or wall (see sketch). Hang pennants on clothesline with clothespins—several clothespins for each child. Place chair and jar toward side of playing area.

Procedure

Ask, **What do you know about (Abraham)?** Volunteer states one fact about Abraham and takes a clothespin from the pennant. (Examples: Abraham lived in Old Testament times. God promised Abraham many grandchildren. Abraham had a wife named Sarah. Abraham had a baby boy and named him Isaac.) The volunteer then kneels on chair and drops the clothespin into the jar. Children take turns stating facts and dropping clothespins into jar until all clothespins are removed and pennant is taken down.

City Statues

Materials Checklist

- [ ] unlined index cards
- [ ] felt pen
- [ ] two rolls of masking tape

Optional—

- [ ] stopwatch

Preparation

If you are reviewing a Bible memory verse, letter the verse on index cards—several words on each card. Draw a simple pigeon shape around the words (sketch a). Make an identical second set of cards.

Procedure

Divide class into two teams. Give each team a set of cards and roll of tape. Have each team choose one of its members to be a city statue. If the verse is especially long, the teams may have more than one statue. Each statue holds arms outstretched while the team races to tape "pigeons" to his or her arms in the correct order (sketch b). Time the teams. The first team to attach all of the cards in the correct order wins. Repeat several times to see if the teams can improve their times.

Ask discussion questions such as, **What is a way you can obey this verse? Which characters in this story showed (respect)?**

b.

a.

Honor your

Dogcatchers

Materials Checklist

- [ ] wide masking tape
- [ ] blue and red felt pens
- [ ] scissors

Preparation

If you are reviewing a Bible memory verse, use blue marker to letter the verse on a strip of tape. Group words in short phrases (sketch a). Use a red marker to letter the words in exactly the same phrases on another strip of tape. Cut the phrases apart.

Procedure

Play this game outdoors or in an indoor area where children can run freely. Divide the class into a blue team and a red team. Have a member of each team volunteer to be a dogcatcher. Have the members of red team tape the red words to the front of their shirts and the blue team members tape the blue words to the front of their shirts (sketch b). These players are all stray dogs and the other team's dogcatcher will try to tag them. Designate two locations to be dog pounds, where dogcatchers will keep the dogs they catch. The dogs must go to that location when they are tagged and they must line up in the order in which the dogcatcher places them. A team wins when its dogcatcher gets all of the other team's dogs in the dog pound in the correct order.

a.

Let love | and | faithfulness

b.

Let love

Howdy, Pardner

Materials Checklist

- [ ] Bible
- [ ] children's music cassette and cassette player
- [ ] index card for each child
- [ ] felt pen

Preparation

Divide index cards into two even stacks—*A* and *B*. On each card in stack *A*, letter the words of the Bible memory verse, leaving out a different word on each card. Letter each missing word onto a card in stack *B*. Shuffle each stack separately.

Procedure

Divide class into two teams—*A* and *B*. Teams line up, facing each other, about 10 feet (3 m) apart. Give each player on Team *A* one card from stack *A*. Give each player on Team *B* one card from stack *B*. Teacher invites first child from team *A* to step forward and read his or her card aloud, using the word "howdy" in place of the missing word. Any player from Team *B* who thinks he or she is holding the missing word may step forward and say the word. If the word is incorrect, child steps back in line. Continue until correct word is found. When correct match is found, teacher plays a song from children's music cassette. The two players lock arms and swing each other around, as the other players clap. When the music stops, the two players quickly return to the front of their lines and weave in and out between team members, hooking elbows (see sketch). All team members sit down when player reaches the end of the line. First team to do so gains a point. Game continues until all cards have been matched. The team with the most points wins.

Barnyard Scramble

Materials Checklist

- [ ] index card for each child
- [ ] felt pen

Optional—

- [ ] animal stickers

Preparation

Divide verse into phrases of two or three words each. Letter each phrase on a separate index card. Make three identical sets of verse cards. Next, draw a sheep on each card in first set. Draw a pig on each card in second set. Draw a cow on each card in third set. (*Optional:* Use animal stickers instead of drawing on cards.) Shuffle all cards together.

Procedure

Give one card to each child. Allow time for children to look at their cards. At the teacher's signal, the children wander around the room making the animal noises indicated on their cards. By listening to animal noises, the children find and gather with like animals. Once complete groups have gathered, members hold cards up so verse is in the correct order. Groups make their animal sounds to signal they are finished. If time allows, collect cards and redistribute to repeat game.

sheep   pig   cow

Be completely humble

and gentle;

be patient

Hiker Search

Materials Checklist

- [ ] large index cards
- [ ] hole punch
- [ ] scissors
- [ ] string
- [ ] felt pen

Preparation

Letter the session's Bible memory verse on index cards—one word on each card. Punch two holes in each card at top edge. Cut string into 2-foot (60-cm) lengths—one for each card. Insert a length of string through holes in each card and knot ends together (see sketch).

Procedure

Choose volunteers to wear verse cards around their necks. They stand in front of class and work together to line up so that words of verse are in order. Read verse aloud with all children.

Then, while children's eyes are closed, ask several volunteers from the memory verse line to hide somewhere in the room or stand outside the door. Children open their eyes and try to guess which words are missing. Hiding children return to the line when their word is called and everyone repeats the verse together. Repeat procedure, removing different words each time. If time allows, choose different volunteers to wear the cards and play game again.

Optional: With a stopwatch, time each group as they try to arrange themselves in correct order. Seek to establish a new, all-time record!

Climbing the Mountain

Materials Checklist

- ☐ Bible
- ☐ two large sheets of poster board
- ☐ construction paper
- ☐ string
- ☐ scissors
- ☐ felt pens
- ☐ transparent tape
- ☐ hole punch
- ☐ game bell

Preparation

Draw a simple mountain shape on each sheet of poster board (see sketch). Draw two simple backpackers on construction paper and cut out (see sketch). Punch a hole at the top and bottom of each mountain (see sketch). Loop string through the holes and tie in back of each poster. Use tape to attach one backpacker figure to each piece of string. (Backpacker should be able to be moved up the mountain as string is pulled from back of mountain.) Letter the numbers 1-10 up the side of each mountain (see sketch). Place game bell on table at front of room.

Procedure

Divide class into two teams. The first player on each team comes forward. Teacher reads Bible memory verse, leaving out one word. The first player to ring the game bell may guess the missing word. If the player guesses correctly, he or she moves the backpacker on his or her team's mountain up to number one. If player guesses incorrectly, other player gets a turn to guess. Repeat, leaving out different words, until one team's backpacker reaches number ten.

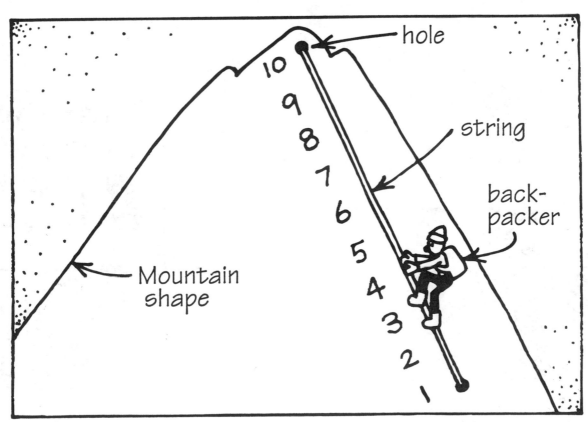

hole

string

back-packer

Mountain shape

Mixed-Up Shoes

Materials Checklist

- [ ] Bible
- [ ] 12 index cards
- [ ] felt pen

Preparation

On each of six index cards, letter the Bible memory verse, leaving out one word. (Leave out a different word on each card.) Then make an identical set of cards.

Procedure

Review Bible memory verse with children. Children remove their shoes and place them in a pile across the room (see sketch). Divide group into two teams. Each team forms a line. Two teachers stand by the shoe pile, each holding a set of index cards.

When teacher says "go," first member of each team runs up to a teacher. The teacher reads the verse written on one of the index cards and the child tells the missing word. If the answer is correct, player may take a shoe from the pile and run back to his or her team. The owner of the shoe puts it on. If the answer is not correct, the player runs back to the line without a shoe. The next player in line takes a turn and teacher reads the next card. (Cards may be reused as necessary.) Play continues until one team has all their shoes on.

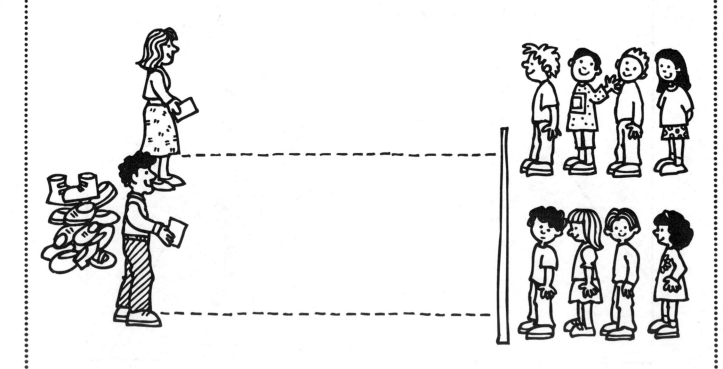

Straw Verse Relay

Materials Checklist

- ☐ four bowls
- ☐ masking tape
- ☐ slips of paper
- ☐ felt pen
- ☐ one drinking straw for each child

Preparation

Letter words of Bible memory verse on slips of paper—one word on each slip. Then make an identical set. Place each set in a separate bowl. Use masking tape to mark starting line. Place two empty bowls on starting line. Place bowls containing verses across the room from starting line.

Procedure

Divide class into two teams. Teams line up behind starting line (see sketch). Give each child a straw. When teacher says "go," first child on each team runs to bowl containing verse, uses straw to lift one slip of paper, runs back to empty bowl and drops paper in. Children in line repeat process until all slips of paper have been transferred to bowl on starting line. Then team members work together to put verse in order. The first team to finish is the winner.

Circle Hop

Materials Checklist

- [ ] children's music cassette and cassette player
- [ ] brightly colored construction paper
- [ ] scissors
- [ ] felt pen
- [ ] paper bag

Preparation

Use scissors to cut large circles from construction paper—two for each child in your class. Use felt pen to number the circles. Place circles randomly on the floor of a carpeted room, not more than 2 feet (.6 m) apart. Cut one small square of paper to correspond to each circle. Number squares and place in paper bag.

Procedure

Play children's music cassette as children step from one circle to another, trying not to touch the floor. When music stops, each child must freeze on a circle. Teacher then draws a number from the bag and reads it out loud. The child standing on the corresponding numbered circle says the day's Bible memory verse. (Choose another number if no child is standing on the number that was read.) If the child has difficulty saying the verse, he or she may choose a friend to help. Play until each child has had an opportunity to say the verse.

Primary/Bible Memory Verse Review

Word Pass

Materials Checklist

- [ ] construction paper
- [ ] felt pen
- [ ] scissors

Preparation

Letter words of Bible memory verse on construction paper and cut verse apart—one word to each section of paper.

Procedure

Children sit in a circle. Pass first word of the verse around the circle. Each child says the word as he or she passes it counterclockwise. The last child in the circle keeps the first word. Pass around the second and following words in the same manner until every word is being held by a different child. Have children hold up words, one at a time, as they say the verse together. Have volunteers say the verse alone.

Dress-Up Relay

Materials Checklist

- [ ] various items of clothing (shirts, jeans, hats, shoes, socks, gloves, coats and dresses)
- [ ] two cardboard boxes
- [ ] masking tape

Preparation

Place a line of masking tape on floor. Place two boxes full of clothes across the playing area from tape.

Procedure

Review the day's Bible memory verse with children. Divide class into two teams. Have each team line up behind the line of masking tape. At a given signal, team members take turns running to box, putting on an item of clothing and running back to the team "dressed up." When everyone on the team has taken a turn, all hold hands and say the Bible memory verse out loud (see sketch). The team to say the verse first is the winner.

For God so loved the world...

Verse Jump

Materials Checklist
☐ long piece of rope

Optional—
☐ stopwatch or timer
☐ chalkboard and chalk

Preparation
None.

Procedure
Review the day's Bible memory verse with children. Have children form a line several yards behind the rope which is held about 1 foot (.3 m) off the ground by two teachers. One at a time, children run and jump over the rope while saying one word of the Bible memory verse. To add excitement, time the group to see how quickly they can complete the entire verse. (*Optional:* If children need help remembering the verse, letter it on the chalkboard so they can refer to it during the game.)

Camel Rider Race

Materials Checklist

- ☐ two foam balls
- ☐ masking tape

Preparation

None.

Procedure

Review the lesson's Bible memory verse with children. Divide group into two equal teams. Give a rubber ball to the first player on each team. At a given signal the "riders" get on their "camels" by putting the ball between their legs and jumping across the play area to where a teacher is waiting. The children say the Bible memory verse and then jump back to their respective teams, passing the ball on to the next players in line. (The teacher may want to prompt children who have difficulty with memorization.) The first team to have all members take a turn wins.

Primary/Bible Memory Verse Review

Buddies

Materials Checklist
☐ cassette tape of lively music
☐ cassette player

Preparation
None.

Procedure
Pair up each child with a buddy. In each pair, call one buddy *A* and the other buddy *B*. All *A*'s form a circle and hold hands. All *B*'s form a circle around the *A*'s and hold hands. As cassette is played, children in circle *A* circle to the left. Children in circle *B* circle to the right. When music stops, children drop hands and quickly find their original buddies. Buddies hold hands and stoop down. When all buddies have stooped, the first pair to squat then stands and says Bible memory verse together.

Pass the Popcorn, Please!

Materials Checklist

☐ popcorn box full of popcorn or caramel corn

Preparation

None.

Procedure

Review the lesson's Bible memory verse with children. Have children stand in a circle. Give popcorn box to one child. Child says the first word of the verse, takes a piece of popcorn to eat and passes the box to the next child. Second child says second word, and so on until verse is completed. The child who is next in the circle gets to say the entire verse. Children continue passing popcorn and saying verse. When the game is over, children may share the remaining popcorn.

Run for It!

Materials Checklist

- [ ] index cards—
  one for each player
- [ ] pen
- [ ] items to build an obstacle
  course, such as a large cardboard box, card table, old
  tires, jump rope, footstool,
  blanket, etc.
- [ ] large playing area

Preparation

Cut the top and bottom from cardboard box. Build an obstacle course, placing items several feet apart. Set box on its side, place tires in a row, place jump rope and footstool on course, set up card table, spread blanket on ground.

Letter Bible memory verse on cards, one word or phrase on each card. Number each card so children will not confuse the order of words. Place cards at the end of obstacle course. (The number of cards should equal the number of players.)

Procedure

Children line up at the start of obstacle course. At a given signal, the first child must:

- crawl through box
- step into each tire
- skip rope five times
- step on and off footstool
- crawl under card table
- roll or somersault across blanket
- pick up card number 1 and run back to line

Children take turns running obstacle course and collecting cards in numerical order until verse is complete. Children then hold up cards and say verse together.

Bop 'n Pop

Materials Checklist

- [ ] balloons
- [ ] small strips of paper
- [ ] felt pen
- [ ] masking tape
- [ ] large cardboard box

Preparation

Letter the lesson's Bible memory verse on strips of paper, one word on each strip. Roll each paper into a cylinder shape and place each one inside a separate balloon. Blow up all balloons and knot, then place them in the box at one end of playing area. (There should be at least one balloon for each player.) Use masking tape to mark a starting line on floor at opposite end of room from box.

Procedure

Children form a line behind masking tape. At a given signal, the first player runs to the box, picks a balloon and "bops" (taps) it back to the starting line. (Player must not carry the balloon or allow it to touch the floor.) When the child has reached the starting line, he or she pops the balloon by sitting on it and finds the rolled-up paper. Next player repeats procedure. Game continues until all balloons have been popped. Players then work together to arrange words in correct order and recite verse.

Primary/Bible Memory Verse Review

Find a Footprint

Preparation

Cut footprints from one color of construction paper—make a footprint for each word in a recent lesson's Bible memory verse. Letter one word on each footprint (see sketch). Make a set of footprints for several recent verses, using a different color of paper for each set. Mix up the four or five sets of footprints and hide them around the room or outside.

Procedure

Divide class into four or five small groups. Assign each group a color. At a given signal, each team begins searching for its own color of footprints. When all its footprints have been found, the team arranges them in order on the floor. Children read the verses together when all have been placed in the proper order.

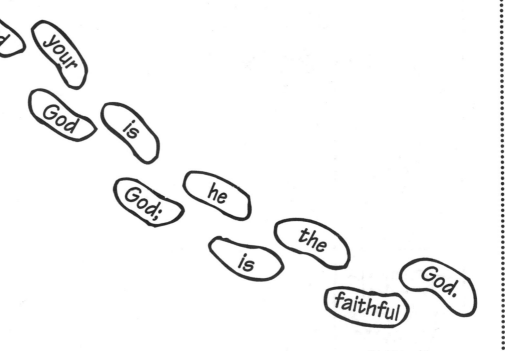

Know therefore that the Lord your God is God; he is the faithful God.

Hopscotch Picto-Verse

Materials Checklist

- [ ] Bible
- [ ] chalk or wide masking tape
- [ ] poster board
- [ ] felt pen

Preparation

Letter the words of memory verse on sheet of poster board. On a paved area outdoors, use chalk to draw a 4×5-foot (1.2×1.5–m) rectangular grid as shown in sketch. Letter words of verse and draw symbolic pictures in squares (Deuteronomy 5:16 is shown). If game is played in classroom, use masking tape to make grid and letter words on tape.

Procedure

Read verse aloud while pointing to words on poster board. Invite children to repeat verse with you. Ask, **What does this verse tell us to do?** Demonstrate jumping from square to square in the appropriate order as you say the words of the verse. Children take turns jumping with two feet in each square while saying the words of the verse. The second time, children hop on one foot.

Variations

For younger children, number the squares or place the words in order on the grid. For larger groups, make several grids. For an added challenge, children jump through grid in pairs.

and	com-manded	you.
your	father	has
mother,	your	Lord your God
Honor	as	the

Primary/Bible Memory Verse Review

Red Light, Green Light and Giant Steps

Materials Checklist

- ☐ Bible
- ☐ two flashlights
- ☐ red and green cellophane or tissue paper
- ☐ two rubber bands
- ☐ slips of paper
- ☐ bowl
- ☐ masking tape
- ☐ pencil

Preparation

Letter each child's name on a separate slip of paper and place papers in bowl. Use rubber bands to secure red cellophane over the end of one flashlight, and green cellophane over the end of the second flashlight. In a large room that can be darkened, use tape to mark a starting line at one end of the room and a finish line at the other end of the room.

Procedure

Read memory verse aloud from Bible. Invite children to repeat verse with you. Ask, **What does this verse tell us to do?** (Children respond.)

Children stand behind starting line. Teacher stands at finish line. Darken room. When teacher turns on green flashlight, students may take giant steps forward. When teacher turns on red flashlight, students must freeze. Students who continue moving on a red light must take one giant step backwards. While red light is on, teacher draws a slip of paper from bowl. Student whose name is drawn may recite the verse and take one giant step forward. (Students should be rewarded for trying, even if verse is not recited perfectly.) First student to reach finish line may control flash lights for next round.

Market Relay

Materials Checklist

- ☐ Bible
- ☐ two toy shopping carts or wagons
- ☐ empty food or beverage containers such as milk cartons or cereal boxes—one for each word of the verse
- ☐ scraps of paper—one for each word of the verse
- ☐ felt pen
- ☐ masking tape
- ☐ two tables

Preparation

Letter each word of memory verse on a separate slip of paper and tape onto food containers (see sketch). Make two sets. (*Optional:* Omit slips of paper and write directly on food containers.) Place the sets of food containers on two separate tables. Use tape to make a starting line about 20 feet (6 m) from tables.

Procedure

Read memory verse aloud from Bible. Invite children to repeat verse with you several times. Have children define several key words.

Divide class into two teams. Teams line up behind starting line. At teacher's signal, first shopper on each team pushes shopping cart to table. Shopper places one food container in cart and pushes cart back to team. Second player then races to get a second food item. When all food items have been retrieved, team puts words of the verse in order.

Variations

For an additional challenge, each shopper must recite verse to a store clerk before buying a food item. Or place all food items in one pile and have students find which word of the verse their team needs.

The Hula Hoop Hustle

Materials Checklist

- [ ] Bible
- [ ] four chairs
- [ ] four hula hoops
- [ ] four sheets of construction paper
- [ ] felt marker
- [ ] tape
- [ ] slips of paper—one for each pair of children
- [ ] four hole punchers

Preparation

Place chairs at four different locations around the room or yard to make hula hoop stations. Place a hula hoop at each station. Letter one of the following instructions on each sheet of construction paper: 1. Stand inside hula hoop with your partner and say the verse. 2. Roll hula hoop back and forth with your partner and say verse. 3. Hold hands with your partner and jump in and out of hula hoop as you say the verse. 4. Twirl hula hoop on your arm or around waist as your partner says verse, then switch. Tape one instruction sheet on each chair (see sketch).

To make tickets, write the numbers 1, 2, 3 and 4 on each slip of paper (see sketch). Arrange for a teacher or helper to punch tickets at each station. (If your group is small, set up only two stations, both with two actions.)

Procedure

Read memory verse aloud from Bible. Invite children to repeat verse with you. Ask, **Why would it be a good idea to obey this verse?** (Children respond.)

Children choose partners. Each pair stands by a different station and is given one ticket. Explain instructions at each station. Pairs carry out instructions at each station and have their ticket punched by teacher or helper before moving on to next station. Pairs may move from station to station in any order, and may need to wait their turn if another pair is already at that station.

Slam Dunk!

Materials Checklist

- [ ] Bible
- [ ] chalk or masking tape
- [ ] two trash cans
- [ ] six traffic cones or other obstacles
- [ ] newspapers

Preparation

Use chalk or masking tape to make a start and finish line about 25 feet (7.5 m) apart. Place trash cans behind finish line, about 10 feet (3 m) apart. Arrange traffic cones between lines to form an obstacle course for each team (see sketch). Crumple newspapers into two large balls.

Procedure

Read memory verse aloud from the Bible. Invite children to repeat verse with you several times. Divide class into two teams. Teams line up behind starting line. First player on each team stands at finish line holding trash can. At teacher's signal, second player on each team runs through obstacle course, carrying ball, and tosses ball into can. Second player then switches places with the first player. First player retrieves the ball, runs backwards through the obstacle course and passes the ball to the third player. Process continues until all team members have had a chance to be the trash can holder. When last player returns, team members recite verse together and sit down.

When game is over say, **It's hard to run backwards! Some of us are good at sports and others are not. Some of us are good at drawing and others are not. Some of us are good at math or writing or playing an instrument. The wonderful thing about God's family is that there is a place for everyone, no matter what you can or can't do. God loves all of us and created each person to be special.**

Crazy Chicken Run

Materials Checklist

- [ ] felt pen
- [ ] large index cards—one for each word in verse
- [ ] masking tape

Preparation

Letter memory verse on cards—one word on each card. Tape cards in visible locations around the room or in an open area outside.

Procedure

Say, **We're going to play a game called "Crazy Chicken Run."**

Children gather in center of room. When teacher says, "Run, crazy chickens, run!," children scatter and run to any card. As soon as a child reaches a card, he or she touches the card and then freezes into a "crazy" position.

More than one child may stand by a card. However, encourage children to spread out evenly, so that every card has at least one child standing by it. As soon as all children are frozen, point to the card with the first word of the verse. Group (or child) standing by card says the word on the card. Point to cards in order, until entire verse has been recited.

Repeat game, allowing children to run to a different card each time. As children become more familiar with verse, point to cards more quickly.

After the game, ask, **What does this verse command us to do?** (Children respond.) **What is one way we can (show love to each other)?** (Volunteers respond.)

"My command is this:

Love

each

other

as I

have

loved

you."

John 15:12

Farmer's Joy Rap

Materials Checklist

- ☐ Bible
- ☐ farmer's hat
- ☐ chalkboard and chalk

Preparation

Letter the words of memory verse on chalkboard. Practice saying the verse rhythmically as indicated in example below. (Clap on words.)

(1) The Lord (clap, clap)
(2) has done (clap, clap)
(3) great things (clap, clap)
(4) for us, (clap, clap)
(5) and we (clap, clap)
(6) are filled (clap, clap)
(7) with joy. (clap, clap)

Procedure

Have children sit in a circle. Demonstrate the rhythmic verse, including claps. Have children join you in saying the verse. When you feel children have become confident, have a volunteer wear farmer's hat and say first line of verse. While child is saying the words, the rest of the children clap to keep rhythm. The child then places the hat on the person sitting to his or her right. That child says the second line of the verse in rhythm. Play continues around circle until every child has had an opportunity to wear hat and verse is completed. (*Optional:* Repeat game, allowing children to create other rhythmic motions to substitute for hand claps.)

Nest Building

Materials Checklist

- ☐ Bible
- ☐ large ball of yarn (preferably brown or yellow)
- ☐ chalk and chalkboard or poster board and felt pen
- ☐ tape or tacks

Preparation

Letter words of memory verse on chalkboard or poster board. Display verse in visible location.

Procedure

Read verse together.

Guide children to sit in a small circle. One child holds the ball of yarn and says the first word of the verse. Holding tightly to the loose end of yarn ball, he or she then tosses the ball to another child, allowing the yarn to unravel. The child who catches the ball of yarn says the next word in the verse. Again, he or she holds on to the unraveling yarn and tosses the yarn ball to another child. Continue process until entire verse has been read. The yarn should form a criss-cross design, similar to a nest. Give help to children as needed. Children rewind yarn before playing again.

Raking Relay

Materials Checklist

- [ ] Bible
- [ ] large open area
- [ ] large sheet of poster board
- [ ] scissors
- [ ] felt pen
- [ ] chalkboard and chalk
- [ ] two leaf rakes (or two brooms)
- [ ] masking tape

Preparation

Letter memory verse on chalkboard. Cut poster board in half. Letter verse on each half of poster board and cut into large jigsaw pieces. (At least one jigsaw puzzle piece is needed for every child.) Place tape on ground (about 20 feet [9m] apart) for start and finish lines.

Procedure

Read verse aloud with children, then erase from chalkboard. Divide class into two teams. Teams line up at starting line. Place a complete memory verse puzzle in a pile near each team. One teacher or helper stands opposite each team, on finish line. Give a rake to the first player on each team. At your signal, player rakes one puzzle piece to finish line. Team member then runs back to team. Relay continues until last player completes verse by placing words in order, and team recites verse together.

Scrambled Eggs

Materials Checklist

- [ ] Bible
- [ ] large frying pan
- [ ] stirring spoon
- [ ] yellow fabric (slightly smaller than frying pan)
- [ ] large sheet of white paper
- [ ] permanent felt pen
- [ ] scissors
- [ ] chalk and chalkboard
- [ ] large plastic egg for each child (pantyhose containers or Easter eggs)

Preparation

Letter the words of memory verse on yellow fabric, on white paper and on the chalkboard. Cut paper verse into as many puzzle pieces as you have children in group (see sketch). Place one puzzle piece in each egg. Hide eggs around the room. Hide yellow fabric in your sleeve or pocket.

Procedure

While children are still seated, say, **Today we are going to make scrambled eggs.** Inform children that there are eggs hidden all around the room. As each child finds an egg, he or she brings the egg to teacher who is holding frying pan. One at a time, children gently tap egg on side of pan and open egg. Placing "eggshells" aside, child reads paper which is now in frying pan. Child then locates his or her section of the verse on the chalkboard, underlines it, and sits down. When last child has underlined his or her part of the verse and everyone is seated, say, **While we're waiting for the eggs to cook, let's read our verse.** Stir "egg" in pan with spoon. Turn your back to the children as you recite verse together. Quickly place yellow fabric in pan so children do not see. Face children and say, **Let's see if the eggs are ready. I think they are!** With spoon, pull up yellow fabric. **Look what we made!** Hold yellow fabric up so children can see the verse. Repeat verse several times. Ask children the meaning of several key words.

"Al	ways	try	to	be	kind
to	ea	ch	ot	her	and
to	ev	ery	one	else	."
1	Thess	alon	ians	5:	15

Verse Tower

Materials Checklist

- [ ] Bible
- [ ] chalkboard and chalk or large sheet of paper and tape or tacks
- [ ] felt pens
- [ ] solid-colored paper cups or Styrofoam cups

Preparation

Letter words of verse on five cups as shown in sketch a. Letter memory verse on the chalkboard or sheet of paper. Place chalkboard or paper in visible location.

Procedure

Read the verse aloud with children. Divide class into groups of three or four. Give each group five cups and a felt pen. Children letter words of verse on cups using your set as a model. Groups then make verse towers (sketch b). If time allows, groups race to put towers together in correct order.

Primary/Bible Memory Verse Review

Pass the Fruit, Please

Materials Checklist

- ☐ Bible
- ☐ children's music cassette and cassette player
- ☐ chalkboard, chalk
- ☐ chalkboard eraser
- ☐ two pieces of fruit (that hang from a tree)

Preparation

Letter memory verse on the chalkboard.

Procedure

Children sit in a circle near chalkboard. Read verse aloud with children. Say, **Ever since God created the first people—Adam and Eve—He has wanted people to know Him and be His friends.** Ask, **What did God give Adam and Eve to eat in the garden? God planted a garden with all kinds of trees that were beautiful and had good food growing on them.** (Show fruit.)

As you play cassette, children pass fruit around circle. When music stops, child holding fruit erases any two words of verse from chalkboard. Then class recites verse. Repeat until all words are erased. Reletter verse on chalkboard. Repeat game, adding second piece of fruit passed in the opposite direction. Each child left holding fruit erases two words.

"Know that the Lord is God. It is he who made us and we are his." Psalm 100:3

Verse Toss

Materials Checklist
- [ ] Bibles
- [ ] chalkboard and chalk or large sheet of butcher paper
- [ ] felt pen and tape or tacks

For every pair of children—
- [ ] one beanbag

Preparation
Letter words of memory verse on the chalkboard or butcher paper.

Procedure
Read verse aloud with children. Divide the class into pairs. Distribute beanbags. Partners play catch, saying one word of the verse each time the beanbag is caught.

Joseph's Hopscotch

Materials Checklist

- ☐ Bible
- ☐ map of Canaan and Egypt
- ☐ chalk or masking tape
- ☐ felt pen
- ☐ flat stones—one for each child

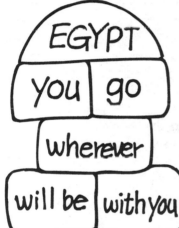

stone

Joseph

Preparation

Make hopscotch grids with chalk outdoors or with masking tape on floor indoors. Make one grid for every four children. Use chalk to letter the words of memory verse inside the squares (see sketch). If indoors, attach a piece of wide masking tape in the center of each square and use felt pen to letter words on the tape. Draw a stick figure of Joseph on each stone.

Procedure

Say, **The Bible tells about a man named Joseph who started out in the land of Canaan and ended up in Egypt.** Point to Canaan and Egypt on map. **God was with Joseph everywhere he went.** Referring to hopscotch grid, read the verse aloud with children. Give a Joseph stone to each child. Demonstrate how to play hopscotch, saying a word of the verse as you hop into each square. Children play Joseph's Hopscotch. When Joseph arrives in Egypt (when child throws Joseph stone into Egypt square), the child recites the entire verse from memory.

Hopscotch Rules: Children line up. First child throws stone into closest square, hops on one foot over that square, then hops into other squares one at a time. Child turns around, hops back and, standing on one foot, picks up stone. Child then throws stone into second square and hops over it to continue game. Child's turn ends when rock lands outside of correct square, or when child steps on a line. Then next player takes a turn. Game continues as children take turns throwing stones into successive squares, hopping over the squares, picking up stones and hopping back. Play until each child has reached the end of the hopscotch.

Marble Tablet

Materials Checklist

☐ Bible

☐ one large stone

☐ sharp pencil

☐ felt pen

For each group of two or three children—

☐ one shirt-size gift box and one marble

Preparation

Use felt pen to draw tablet shape inside box (see sketch). Use the pencil to poke five holes in tablet. Insert your fingertip into each hole to enlarge it. (Holes should be large enough for marble to rest in but not drop through.) Letter one word of the memory verse below each hole and letter "start" in the bottom right hand corner. Make one game for every two or three children. (*Optional:* have children letter words on tablets.)

Procedure

Children pass large stone around as you ask, **Have you ever seen anything carved out of stone?** (Tombstones, statues, sculptures.) **The Bible tells us that God wrote the Ten Commandments on stone tablets.** Divide class into groups of two or three. Distribute game and a marble to each group. Recite verse with the class. In groups, children take turns playing Marble Tablet. First marble is placed in corner marked "start" and child tilts box until marble rests in hole by first word of verse. Child continues until the marble has rested in all holes in the correct order.

Water Xylophone Praises

Materials Checklist

- ☐ Bible
- ☐ chalk and chalkboard or large sheet of paper and felt pen
- ☐ six glass drinking glasses or tall jars
- ☐ water
- ☐ metal spoon
- ☐ masking tape
- ☐ fine-tip felt pen

Preparation

Line up the glasses in a row and fill them with decreasing levels of water as in sketch.

Tap the glasses with a metal spoon. From left to right they should make the first six notes of the musical scale (do, re, mi, fa, sol, la). To lower the pitch, add water; to raise the pitch, remove some water. Place tape on the outside of each glass at the water level. Letter the words of the memory verse and numbers on tape as shown in sketch. As the glasses are tapped in numbered order (which puts the memory verse in order), they should play "Twinkle, Twinkle, Little Star." Letter memory verse on chalkboard or large sheet of paper.

Procedure

Today we're going to play a water xylophone and sing our memory verse to the tune of "Twinkle, Twinkle, Little Star." Demonstrate how to tap each glass and sing the words taped to the front of the glass. Children take turns tapping out tune on water xylophone while class sings the memory verse. (*Optional:* Children make up melodies and tap them on glasses while saying words of verse.) Ask, **Why do you think it is good to sing praises to God?** (Volunteers answer.) **God is good and loving. It is good when we show our love for God by thanking and praising Him.**

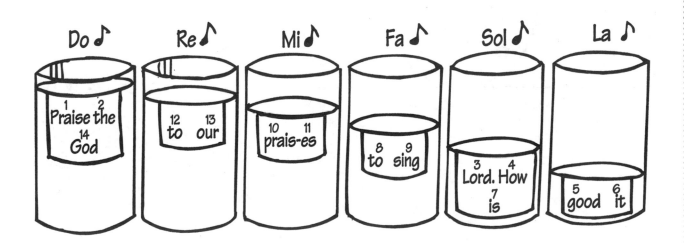

Straw in the Manger

Materials Checklist

- [ ] Bible
- [ ] chalkboard and chalk or large sheet of butcher paper
- [ ] large sheet of poster board
- [ ] felt pens
- [ ] sharp pencil or awl
- [ ] masking tape

For each child—

- [ ] one yellow chenille wire (pipe cleaner)

Preparation

On the center of poster board, sketch a simple drawing of baby Jesus in the manger (sketch a). Do not draw straw in manger. Instead, use pencil or awl to poke holes around baby where children can insert chenille wire "straw." Fold down sides of poster board and tape to table or floor (sketch b). Letter memory verse on the chalkboard or butcher paper. Hide chenille wires throughout the room.

Procedure

Repeat verse aloud with children. Point to manger. Ask, **Do you notice something missing from this manger?** (Straw.) **When you think you can say the verse from memory, you may hunt for "straw" in our classroom. When you find a piece of straw** (show a pipe cleaner), **bring it to me. If you can say the memory verse, you may put the straw in the manger.** Children find and insert "straw" in manger.

Variation: Cut the wires into different lengths. Instead of hiding wires, hold them in your hand so they look the same length and let each child choose one. The child with the longest wire recites verse first and inserts "straw" in manger. Children take turns in order, according to the length of their wires.

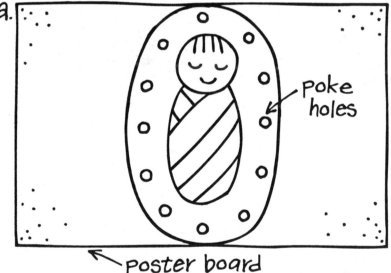

a.

Poke holes

poster board

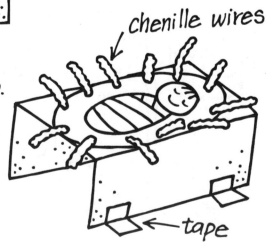

chenille wires

b.

tape

Never-Ending Circles

Materials Checklist

- ☐ Bible
- ☐ chalkboard and chalk or large sheet of butcher paper
- ☐ felt pens
- ☐ scissors
- ☐ 2-liter bottle
- ☐ sand or unpopped popcorn kernels

For each child—

- ☐ one large paper plate

Preparation

Cut out the center of each paper plate, forming a ring that will easily fit over the bottle (sketch a). Letter memory verse on the chalkboard or butcher paper. Fill bottle with sand or popcorn kernels and set bottle on the floor.

Procedure

Children letter the Bible Memory Verse on their rings. Ask, **Can you find the end of your circle?** (No.) **A circle doesn't have an end. Eternal life doesn't have an end, either—it lasts forever. God gives life that lasts forever to people who believe in Jesus.**

Children form a line several feet away from bottle. Children take turns reciting verse and tossing rings over bottle (sketch b).

a.

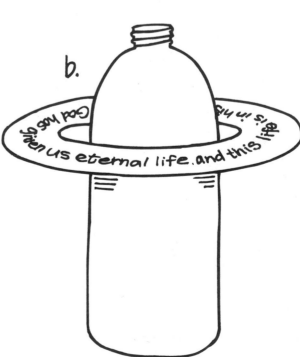

b.

Verse Relays

Materials Checklist

☐ Bible

☐ chalkboard and chalk or large sheet of butcher paper and felt pen

☐ tape or tacks

☐ two elasticized fabric headbands

Preparation

Letter the memory verse on chalkboard or butcher paper.

Procedure

Read verse aloud with children. Divide class into two teams. Team 1 lines up across from teacher. Team 2 lines up across from second teacher or helper (see sketch).

Bible memory verse is displayed where children may refer to it during relay. Teams compete in three relays. In the first relay, players hop on one foot to teachers, recite memory verse and hop back to teams. In the second relay, players use headbands as blindfolds, find their way to teachers, recite verse, take off headbands and run back to teams. (Teachers may help guide blindfolded children by giving verbal directions.) In the third relay, children run to teacher, recite verse and run back to teams. Ask, **Which relay was most difficult? Which was easiest? Our bodies work best when we can use *all* parts. Just like each part of our bodies has a job to do, each person in God's family has a job to do. Another name the Bible uses for God's family is the Body of Christ. All the people who love Jesus are like parts of His body. Each of us has a special job to do to help God's family.** Point out various talents individual children have and how these talents might be used in God's family. For example, **Lindsey likes talking to people. She can tell people about Jesus. Mark likes to sing. He can use his voice to praise God. Eric always has a smile on his face. He can cheer up people who are sad.**

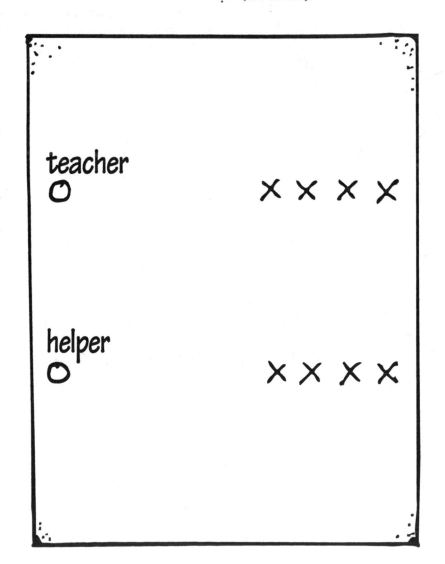

teacher
O
✗ ✗ ✗ ✗

helper
O
✗ ✗ ✗ ✗

Verse Pop-Up

Materials Checklist

- [ ] Bible
- [ ] index cards
- [ ] felt pen
- [ ] stopwatch or watch with a second hand

Preparation

Letter words of memory verse on index cards—one word on each card.

Procedure

Distribute Verse Cards to children—one or two cards to each child. Review unfamiliar words with children. Read verse aloud several times with children. Sitting in a circle, children recite the verse, each child in turn "popping up" (quickly standing) and saying the word on his or her card. Use stopwatch or watch to determine how quickly the group recites the verse using the pop-up method. Children exchange cards and attempt to beat their former time.

Rocky Creek Verse Game

Materials Checklist

- ☐ Bible
- ☐ blue crepe paper
- ☐ gray construction paper
- ☐ scissors
- ☐ felt pen
- ☐ masking tape

Preparation

Cut rock shapes from construction paper—one for each word of verse. Letter memory verse on rock shapes—one word on each rock. (If class is large make two sets.) Twist blue crepe paper and tape to floor creating creek area (see sketch).

Procedure

From your Bible, read the memory verse to children. Have volunteers tape rocks in creek, in the correct order. Children take turns stepping on rocks as the rest of the class repeats verse. Allow each child to have a second turn, this time jumping from rock to rock.

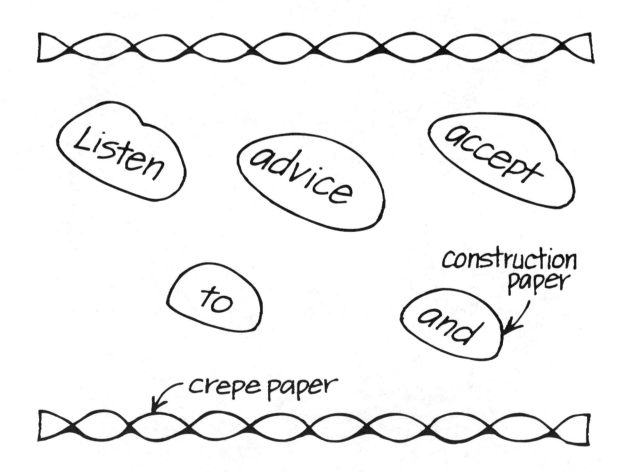

A Verse with Volume

Materials Checklist

☐ chalk and chalkboard or large sheet of paper

☐ felt pens and tape or tacks

Preparation

Letter memory verse on chalkboard or paper, dividing it into four parts as in sketch.

Procedure

Read verse with children. Then together with children, plan a different way to say and act out each of the four parts of the verse. For example, as you say the words "A gentle answer," you may want to use a soft voice and make the motion of petting a kitten. For the words "harsh word," you may want to yell and clap your hands together. Practice saying the verse using the motions and voice inflections you planned.

A gentle answer	turns away wrath,
but a harsh word	stirs up anger.

Proverbs 15:1

Hikers' March

Materials Checklist
☐ Bible
☐ chalkboard and chalk

Preparation
Letter memory verse on chalkboard.

Procedure
Say, **Let's pretend we're going on a hike.** Children form a line and march in place as if hiking. Assist children in keeping time with one another. Then teach children the memory verse, saying it in rhythm with children's steps (see sketch). Children repeat phrases after you. When children are familiar with the verse, march around room while reciting verse.

L R   L   R   L
Do not with-hold good from

R   L   R   L
those who deserve it, when

R   L   R   L   R
it is in your power to act.

Verse Puzzler

Materials Checklist

- [ ] poster board
- [ ] felt pens
- [ ] scissors
- [ ] glue

Preparation

Letter the memory verse on a large sheet of poster board, leaving out four key words (sketch a). Letter missing words on small pieces of poster board. Use a different colored felt pen to letter each word. Cut each word into several puzzle pieces (sketch b). Hide puzzle pieces around room or yard.

Procedure

Divide class into four groups. Assign each group to search for a specific color of puzzle pieces. Groups find puzzle pieces and work together to spell words. A volunteer from each group glues his or her word puzzle in its place on the memory verse poster.

a.

"There is deceit in the
_____ of those who
plot_____ ,but_____
for those who promote
_____ ." Proverbs 12:20

b.

Verse Stations

Materials Checklist

- ☐ Bible
- ☐ paper
- ☐ stickers
- ☐ tape or tacks
- ☐ jump rope
- ☐ small exercise trampoline or pogo ball
- ☐ rubber ball
- ☐ book

For each child—

- ☐ one index card

Preparation

Prepare signs as in sketch. Attach signs to walls at different stations throughout room. Place appropriate props at each station. Arrange to have a teacher or helper at each station to listen to verses.

Procedure

Give each child an index card. Children visit each verse station and follow instructions on signs. The station helpers give out stickers to children who complete the assigned tasks. Children place stickers on index cards. When children have visited all the stations, lead them in reciting the verse together.

Jump rope as you recite, "Trust in the Lord."

Jump on the trampoline as you recite, "with all your heart."

Bounce the ball as you recite, "and he will make."

Balance a book on your head as you recite, "your paths straight."

Find Proverbs 3:5,6 in the Bible and read it aloud.

Primary/Bible Memory Verse Review

Clothespin Relay

Materials Checklist

- [ ] Bible
- [ ] clothespins—2 for each word of the verse
- [ ] index cards—2 for each word of the verse
- [ ] heavy string
- [ ] felt pens
- [ ] scissors
- [ ] tacks

Optional—

- [ ] kitchen timer

Preparation

Cut two 8-foot (2.4-m) lengths of heavy string. Hang lengths of string in classroom to form two "clotheslines." Letter the memory verse and reference on index cards (one word on each card). Make two sets. Mix up the order of cards in each set.

Procedure

Read memory verse from Bible. Repeat verse aloud with children several times. Divide the class into two groups. Each group lines up in front of a clothesline. Place a set of memory verse cards and half of the clothespins in front of each group. The first child in each line picks up the first card in the pile and hangs it on the line. The next child in each line picks up the next card and hangs it up in correct relation to the first word. Game continues until each team has the whole verse hanging in order on the string. (*Optional:* Set a kitchen timer for appropriate amount of time. Teams try to complete verse before timer rings.)

Sharing Badge

Materials Checklist

- [ ] Bible
- [ ] paper
- [ ] poster board
- [ ] scissors
- [ ] ruler
- [ ] paper bag
- [ ] glue
- [ ] felt markers
- [ ] masking tape
- [ ] safety pins
- [ ] photocopy machine

Preparation

Cut 3-inch (7.5-cm) circles from poster board—one for each child. Draw a 2-inch (5-cm) circle on paper and letter the memory verse inside. Photocopy and cut out—one for each child. Letter each child's name on a separate slip of paper and place in paper bag.

Procedure

Read memory verse from the Bible. Repeat verse aloud with children. Then each child draws a slip of paper from the bag. Each child makes a badge for the person whose name he or she drew (see sketch). Children give badges to the classmates for whom they were made. **You all shared with someone today. Sharing is one way God wants us to show love for others.**

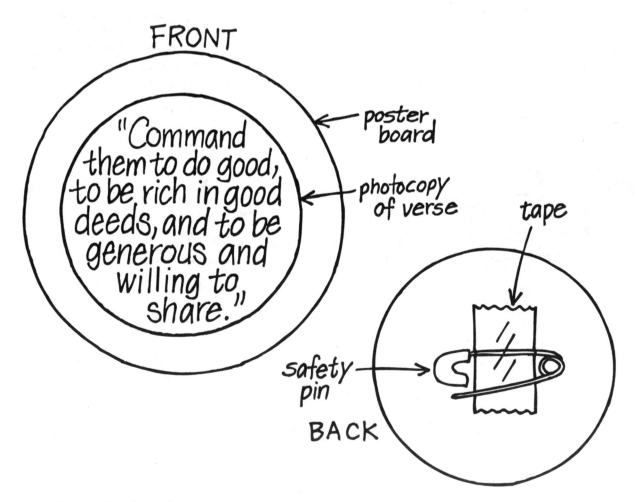

FRONT — poster board — photocopy of verse — "Command them to do good, to be rich in good deeds, and to be generous and willing to share."

tape — safety pin — BACK

Memory Verse Canvas

Materials Checklist

- [ ] Bible
- [ ] butcher paper
- [ ] scissors
- [ ] felt markers
- [ ] crayons
- [ ] masking tape or tacks

Preparation

Cut a long strip of butcher paper. Using block letters, write the memory verse on the paper (see sketch). Lay the butcher paper on a long table or floor of classroom. (*Optional:* Write each letter on a separate piece of paper. Each child colors in one letter and hangs it on the wall in the appropriate place.)

Procedure

Read verse with children. Then children use crayons or felt pens to color in the letters of the verse. Hang completed poster on the wall or bulletin board.

If you love me, you will obey what I command. John 14:15

Verse Teamwork

Materials Checklist
- ☐ chalkboard and chalk or five sheets of paper
- ☐ felt pen and tape

Preparation
Letter memory verse on chalkboard or sheets of paper as shown in sketch.

Procedure
Divide class into five groups. Each group crouches together in front of one section of the verse (see sketch). As you point to the first group they quickly stand, say their portion of the verse, and crouch down again. Continue pointing to each group in order. Have groups change places and repeat.

"God... wants all men   to be saved   and to come to a knowledge   of the truth."   1 Timothy 2:4

Primary/Bible Memory Verse Review

Verse Variety

Materials Checklist
- ☐ Bible
- ☐ chalkboard, chalk and eraser

Preparation
Letter the memory verse on the chalkboard.

Procedure
Read the verse aloud with children. Ask volunteer to erase one word of the verse. Then class reads verse, filling in the missing word. Children take turns erasing words. After each word is erased, the class reads the verse aloud, filling in the missing words. Each time you read the verse suggest a different way to read it. (Whisper, slowly, quickly, while standing on one foot, etc.) Continue until all words have been erased and children have said the entire verse from memory.

"Trust in the Lord and /// good."

Psalm 37:3

Bible Verse Treasure Sack

Materials Checklist

- [ ] yellow or gold felt squares
- [ ] black felt pen
- [ ] scissors
- [ ] brown paper sack

Preparation

To make coins: Cut felt into 10 to 12 circles, varying in size from two to four inches (5 to 10cm) in diameter. Letter one or two words of the memory verse on each coin. Number coins on reverse side (see sketch). Place coins in sack.

Procedure

There's a message hidden in this treasure sack. See if you can discover what it is! Children work together to put verse in order. If children are beginning readers, they may place the coins in numerical order, then turn the coins over to discover verse. Advanced readers may refer to the numbers to check their work. When verse is in order, read it with children. To help children learn the verse, volunteers may put one circle at a time back in the treasure sack, repeating the verse and supplying missing words each time a circle is removed.

Verse Rhythm

Materials Checklist

None.

Preparation

Practice saying the memory verse rhythmically, emphasizing underlined words or syllables and clapping where indicated by *x*'s (as shown in example below).

Procedure

Demonstrate to the class the rhythmic memory verse. Have children join you in saying the verse. As children become confident, say the verse faster.

If I *give* all I *possess*

to the <u>poor</u>, x x x

But have not <u>love</u>, x x x

I gain <u>no</u>thing. x x x

Bible Verse Treasure Hunt

Materials Checklist

- [ ] construction paper in two colors
- [ ] felt pen
- [ ] scissors

Preparation

Cut several gem shapes of varying sizes from one color of construction paper. Letter one word of memory verse on each gem (see sketch). Number gem shapes on reverse side. Make another set of lettered and numbered gems, using a different color of paper. Hide both sets of gem shapes around the room.

Procedure

Divide class into two teams. Assign each team a color corresponding to a set of gems. Instruct each team to search for its colored gems. Then each team works together to put the verse in order. When teams are finished, recite verse with class. Then allow each team to say the verse aloud.

Bible Memory Verse Puzzle

Materials Checklist

- ☐ Bible
- ☐ four different colors of construction paper
- ☐ felt pen
- ☐ scissors
- ☐ index card

Preparation

Cut each color of paper into a different geometric shape (circle, triangle, square, rectangle). Letter memory verse on shapes (see sketch). Cut each shape into three or four pieces. Underline the Bible Memory Verse in Bible or letter it on index card.

Procedure

Distribute the puzzle pieces to the children. Say, **Find other children with puzzle pieces the same color as yours. Put your puzzle pieces together to make a shape. A word is printed on each shape. Put the words in the same order as the ones I have underlined in the Bible** (or printed on the card)**. You will discover something very important.** Children complete the activity.

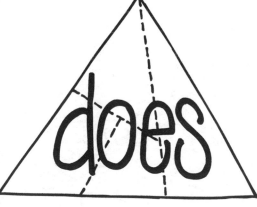

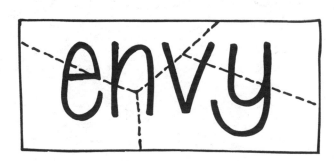

Verse Footprints

Materials Checklist
☐ chalk

Preparation

In an outside area, draw footprints on the ground—one footprint for each word in the memory verse. Letter the memory verse, one word in each footprint (see sketch).

Procedure

Children line up behind footprints, then take turns stepping on footprints as they say the words of the verse. When children become familiar with verse, have them step on footprints as quickly as possible.

Hunting for a Treasure

Materials Checklist

- [ ] nine different-colored sheets of construction paper
- [ ] small index card
- [ ] felt pen
- [ ] scissors

Preparation

Cut each color of paper into a different shape—a boat, a star, a fish, a kite, a truck, a rainbow, a tree, a house and a seashell (see sketch). Letter a different word or phrase from the memory verse on each shape. Place the shapes in view around the room. Letter the following one-word clues on an index card for your own reference. 1. sail; 2. twinkle; 3. swim; 4. fly; 5. putt-putt-putt; 6. colors; 7. beach (or seashore); 8. walls; 9. leaves.

Procedure

As each child arrives, whisper a clue in his or her ear. Write child's name beside each clue as you give it. After you have given the clue explain to the child that he or she is to find the shape that best matches the clue. When all shapes have been found, the group works together to unscramble the message. Recite the memory verse together.

Animal Families

Materials Checklist

☐ chalkboard and chalk, or butcher paper and felt pen

Preparation

None.

Procedure

Lead a short discussion about families by asking questions such as, **How many people are in your family? Does every family have the same number of people? What does your family like to do together? Does every family do the same things together?**

Tell the children the name of an animal that they are to imitate, such as a dog. When you give a signal (such as turning off the lights) children walk around the room, pretending to be dogs. When you give a second signal (such as turning on the lights) the children must freeze. Call out a number such as three, at which point children must quickly form families of three dogs. After all children have formed families, count the number of dog families and the number of dogs left over and record on your butcher paper. Repeat game several times, using different animals and different numbers for family groupings. End by asking children to tell what they like about being in a small or large family.

Fast Farmer Relay

Materials Checklist

- [ ] two pairs of big farm boots
- [ ] two straw hats
- [ ] butcher paper
- [ ] felt pens
- [ ] masking tape
- [ ] "farm" obstacles such as bridge (table), gate (broom braced between two chairs), pumpkin patch (cones on the floor), etc.

Preparation

Set up two identical obstacle courses (see sketch). Attach large sheet of butcher paper to wall at the end of each course. Place felt pens near paper. Use masking tape to mark starting line.

Procedure

Ask, **What might make a person feel happy or joyful?** Volunteers answer. **In our game today, you will have a chance to draw something that makes you feel joyful.** Suggest children think of answer before game begins. Divide group into two even teams. Each team forms a line behind the masking tape. A teacher or helper stands at the end of each obstacle course.

When the teacher says "go," the first member of each team puts on a straw hat and a pair of boots, then runs through the obstacle course to the sheet of butcher paper. The child draws something that makes him or her feel joyful. He or she then runs back to the starting line, places the hat on the next team member and takes off boots. The next child puts on boots and begins obstacle course. Game continues until each child has had a turn. Teams then guess what the other team's pictures show.

Note: This game may be used with any fruit of the Spirit (i.e. children draw ways to show love, peace, patience, etc.).

Flower Power

Materials Checklist

- [ ] children's music cassette and cassette player
- [ ] brightly colored construction paper
- [ ] scissors
- [ ] glue
- [ ] 10 tongue depressors
- [ ] shoebox or Styrofoam base
- [ ] felt pen
- [ ] tape
- [ ] chair for each child

Preparation

Cut flowers from construction paper and glue to tongue depressor stems. On back of each tongue depressor, write one of the following letters: *B,C,D,L,M,P,R,S,T,W.* Insert each flower into the bottom of shoebox or Styrofoam base to make a "flower garden" (see sketch). Cut a larger flower from construction paper and tape to the back of a chair. Place all chairs in a circle around flower garden.

Procedure

Children sit in chairs. When the music begins, the lights are turned off and children walk around inside circle of chairs. When the music stops, the lights are turned on and each child sits down in the chair he or she is closest to. Child sitting in chair marked with the flower picks a flower out of the flower garden. The teacher asks the child to finish one of the following sentences, beginning with a word that starts with the letter on the back of the flower: I can show kindness to my brother or sister by...(letting her choose which TV show to watch); I can show kindness to my mom or dad by...; I can show kindness to the kids at school by.... Child puts flower back in garden. Continue playing until each child has had the opportunity to pick a flower.

You may vary this game for use with a variety of lessons by having child finish the sentence, "I can be patient when..." or "God's peace can help me not to worry when..." etc.

Rocky Review

Materials Checklist

☐ felt pens
☐ glue
☐ outdoor playing area
☐ chalk

For each player—

☐ medium-sized rock with flat bottom
☐ index card

Preparation

On index cards, letter simple questions about the life application of Bible stories. (Remember to use short, easy words.) Glue cards to the bottoms of rocks—one for each child (see sketch). Hide rocks in play area. Use chalk to letter a word from your lesson (such as love, forgive, etc.) on a paved section of play area.

Procedure

Each child searches for a rock and stands next to the one he or she has found. Call on individual children to pick up their rocks and answer the question lettered on the bottom. (Be ready to help beginning readers.) After each child answers question, he or she places rock on chalk lines, spelling the word you lettered. Continue game until each child has had a turn to answer the question on his or her rock. Then children gather where you have spelled out the word.

rock

What is a way to serve a friend?

What happens when we use harsh words?

Primary/Life Application

Whisperin' Messages

Materials Checklist
- ☐ writing paper
- ☐ pencils

Preparation
None.

Procedure
Divide group into teams of six to eight. Each team forms a line. Place several sheets of paper and a pencil at the end of each line. Teacher whispers a phrase to the first person in each line, telling something that God wants His family to do (i.e., God wants us to share). The teams then whisper the phrase from person to person until the last person on the team has received the message. He or she then writes the message on a slip of paper, hands it to the teacher and goes to the front of the line. Any team that has written the correct phrase earns 10 points. (Spelling errors should be overlooked.) Play again using a different message. (*Optional:* The last child in each line whispers the message to the teacher instead of writing it.)

God's Family Letter Game

Materials Checklist

- ☐ felt pen
- ☐ chalk and chalkboard
- ☐ scissors

For each group of four children—

- ☐ 15 index cards

Preparation

Cut index cards in half. Letter the following words onto cards, one letter on each card—share, help, tell, care, love, pray. On the five extra cards, letter a, e, r, l and *. Make a set of cards for each group of four children.

Procedure

Ask children to name things God wants people in His family to do. Write these words on chalkboard. (Share, help, tell, care, love, pray.) Divide class into groups of four. Give each group a set of alphabet cards. Each child takes five cards. Children place cards face up in front of them. Remaining cards are placed face down in a pile. Place one card face up to begin a discard pile. First child draws one card from either pile and then places a card face up on the discard pile. Play continues as each child takes a turn, attempting to collect the cards necessary to spell one of the words listed on the chalkboard. The card marked with a * may be used for any letter. The first child to spell a word is the winner. Children may want to keep playing until everyone has spelled a word. Lead children in a discussion of the words they spelled by asking questions such as, **What are some ways people in God's family can show they care?**

Puppet Pals

Materials Checklist

- ☐ three puppets
- ☐ table or other prop to use as puppet stage

Preparation

None.

Procedure

Invite three children at a time to come up and use puppets as class looks on. Teacher interacts with puppets, setting the stage for a brief skit in which the puppets act out an application of the day's Bible lesson (such as being kind or helpful). For example, the teacher might say, "Oh, my, I spilled all the crayons. I don't know what to do!" The puppets would then act out helping the teacher pick up the crayons. The teacher can end the skit by saying, "Thank you! You obeyed God by being helpful today!" Continue until all students have had an opportunity to use puppets, using a different situation for each skit.

Primary/Life Application

Wonder Words

Materials Checklist

- [ ] several medium paper bags
- [ ] fine sandpaper
- [ ] scissors
- [ ] chalkboard
- [ ] chalk

Preparation

Cut letters from sandpaper to spell key words from lesson. (E.g., - WISE, HEAR, LEARN.) Place the letters for each word in a separate paper bag.

Procedure

Say, **We are going to spell an important word from our lesson today. The word is (wise).** Letter the word on the chalkboard. Have a volunteer place his or her hand in the appropriate paper bag, "feel" for the letter **W** and take it out. Ask, **What letter comes next?** Another child selects the letter **I** from bag without looking. Continue until word is spelled. Child who takes the last letter from bag says the word and uses it in a sentence. Ask, **What does it mean to be wise?** Repeat procedure for each bag of letters.

Middler
Games

Street Corners

Materials Checklist

- [ ] poster board
- [ ] red and green construction paper
- [ ] two rulers
- [ ] felt pen
- [ ] scissors
- [ ] paper
- [ ] pencil
- [ ] tape

Preparation

To make street signs, cut and letter poster board as shown in sketch a. Tape street signs in four different corners of your class-room. Cut red and green con-struction paper into matching octagon shapes. Letter "Stop" on red paper and "Go" on green paper. Tape a ruler onto each octagon to make "Stop" and "Go" signs (sketch b).

On a sheet of paper, list several "what, where, why and who" questions about the session's Bible story (sketch c). Make an even amount of each type of question.

Procedure

Divide class into four teams. Teacher stands in center of room and holds "Go" sign while teams walk around perimeter of room without touching. At any time, teacher may discreetly change sign to "Stop." As soon as children notice "Stop" sign, teams run to the nearest corner and sit down. (each team must be in a different corner.) The first team to have all its members seated at the same corner receives one point. Once all the teams are seated, the teacher asks each team a question that corresponds with its street sign. If the team answers cor-rectly, it gets one point. If answer is incorrect, second team gets a chance to answer question. Play resumes when teacher holds up "Go" sign. Game continues until all the questions have been answered. Team with the most points wins.

a.

WHAT ST.

WHERE AVE.

WHY RD.

WHO DR.

b.

ruler

c.

What did Jonathan and David do when they said good-bye?

Where did David hide from Saul?

Who did David marry?

Why did Saul want to kill David?

Chopstick Relay

Materials Checklist

- [ ] Bible
- [ ] two large bowls
- [ ] three Chinese take-out food containers
- [ ] felt pen
- [ ] paper
- [ ] pencil
- [ ] table
- [ ] chalkboard and chalk or large sheet of paper

For each child—

- [ ] Ping-Pong ball or large marshmallow
- [ ] a set of chopsticks

Preparation

Choose a Bible story students have studied. On a sheet of paper, list true or false statements about events in the Bible story—one statement for every two students. Include several statements which do not relate to the story. (Examples: Ruth was Naomi's daughter-in-law [T]; Ruth and Naomi moved to Egypt [F]; Naomi loved to sew [NIS]). Letter one container "True," one "False," and one "Not in Story" (sketch a). Place an even amount of Ping-Pong balls in each bowl. Place containers on table at one side of room, bowls on the floor across the room.

Procedure

Divide class into two equal teams. (If you have an extra student, he or she may read aloud the true or false statements and keep score.) Teams line up between bowls and containers as shown in sketch b. Give each player a set of chopsticks.

Teacher reads aloud a statement about the Bible story and says, "Go!" Player at the head of each line uses chopsticks to pick up a Ping-Pong ball. (Use marshmallows if ping-pong balls are difficult for your students to handle.) He or she then passes ball to next player with chopsticks. Ball is passed most effectively if it rests on top of chopsticks (sketch c). Procedure continues until ball reaches the end of the line. The last player carries the ball with the chopsticks and drops it into the appropriate food container. Player then goes to the head of the line. The first student to put the Ping-Pong ball in the correct container scores a point for his or her team. In case of a tie, each team scores a point. Repeat process until all players have had a turn. Teacher records each team's score on chalkboard or large sheet of paper. Ask, **What part of this story is the most important? Why? What did you learn from this story?**

a. TRUE FALSE NOT IN STORY

b.

c.

Community Chaos

Materials Checklist

- [ ] Bible
- [ ] 20 large index cards
- [ ] felt pen

Preparation

Choose a Bible story or Bible memory verse students have studied. List 10 events from the story (or words from verse)—one event (or word) on each card (sketch a). Make two identical sets of cards.

Procedure

Divide class into two teams. Teams line up as in sketch b. Shuffle both sets of cards together and spread all cards facedown on the floor between teams.

Assign each child on one team a city occupation (bus driver, firefighter, police officer, librarian, doctor, barber, teacher, hairstylist, baker, crossing guard, etc.). Assign players on other team the same occupations. To begin play, call out a job description such as "I drive people from one place to another." each of the two children who have that occupation quickly choose any one of the cards on the floor and brings it back to his or her team. Repeat process by calling out another job description. As children bring cards to their teams, team members try to place their cards in the correct story sequence or word order. If a child brings a duplicate card, player who is called next returns card to pile before choosing a new card. Team which first places all the cards in the correct order wins. Discuss the Bible story by asking questions such as, **Which of these events was the most important? Why? What did the characters from this story demonstrate? How?**

a.

Jesus visited Mary and Martha.

Martha cleaned the house.

Mary talked to Jesus.

Martha became angry.

Jesus loves both Mary and Martha.

Jesus was arrested and crucified.

Mary and Martha were sad and cried.

Jesus rose from the dead.

Jesus died so we could be forgiven

Each person has a special place in God's family.

b.

bus driver

baker

police officer

grocer

barber

barber

grocer

police officer

baker

bus driver

Chair Scramble

Materials Checklist

- [ ] Bible
- [ ] chairs
- [ ] paper
- [ ] pencil
- [ ] large index cards
- [ ] tape

Preparation

Choose a Bible story students have studied. On a sheet of paper, list true or false statements about events in the Bible story. List one statement for every two children in your group. Letter one index card "True" and another "False." Tape labeled index cards to chairs (sketch a).

Procedure

Divide class into two equal teams. (If you have an extra student, he or she may read aloud the true or false statements.) Teams sit on floor as shown in sketch. Assign each child a number (sketch b).

After teams are seated, leader reads aloud a statement about the Bible story and then calls out a number. The students from each team with that number jump up and run to sit in their team's "true" or "false" chair. The student who sits in the correct chair first scores a point for his or her team. In case of a tie, each team scores a point. Repeat process until all true or false statements have been read. Pause to allow students to correct each false statement. Repeat game as time permits.

b.

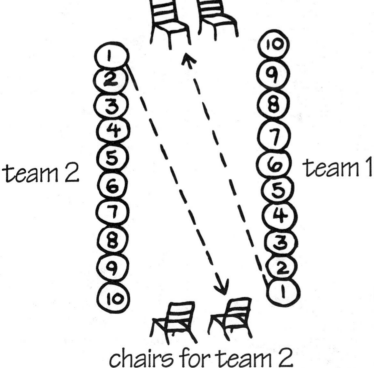

chairs for team 1

team 2

team 1

chairs for team 2

a.

True   False

Fruit Pop

Materials Checklist

- ☐ Bible
- ☐ small strips of paper
- ☐ pen
- ☐ yellow, orange, red, purple and green balloons
- ☐ large plastic garbage bags

Preparation

Choose a Bible story students have studied. List 10 events from the story, 1 event on each strip of paper (see sketch). Roll strips and insert into each balloon. Inflate balloons and tie. Put balloons into a large plastic bag. Make an identical set of balloons for each team of six to eight students. (*Optional:* Make one set of all orange balloons and label bag "oranges." Make another set of purple balloons and label bag "grapes," etc.)

Procedure

Divide class into teams of six to eight students each. Give each team a plastic bag with balloons. At your signal, students remove balloons from bag, pop them and put the Bible story events in the correct sequence. (If a child has a negative reaction to popping balloons, allow him or her the choice of not participating, or helping only with the sequencing.) After all teams have put their strips in order, discuss the Bible story by asking questions such as, **Which of these events was the most important? Why? What do you learn about God from this story? Which character showed (kindness)? How?**

> Jesus talks to a lawyer.

> Jesus tells a story.

> Jewish man takes a trip.

> Robbers beat Jewish man.

> Jewish man waits for help.

> Priest ignores man.

> Levite ignores man.

> Samaritan bandages man's cuts.

> Samaritan takes man to inn.

> Jesus tells lawyer, "Be kind like the Samaritan."

Ball Toss

Materials Checklist

- [ ] Bible
- [ ] three baskets or boxes
- [ ] a small index card for each child
- [ ] felt pen
- [ ] softball or beanbag
- [ ] three large index cards
- [ ] tape
- [ ] large sheet of paper or chalkboard and chalk

Preparation

Letter three large index cards: "True," "False," and "Not in Story." Attach each index card to a basket or box. On each small index card write a statement about the Bible story that can be identified as "true" or "false." Include several statements which do not relate to the story. (*Optional:* You may choose to make more than one card for each child.)

Procedure

Divide class into two teams. Teams line up 6-8 feet (1.8-2.4 m) from the three baskets or boxes. One child may act as scorekeeper. First player on one team chooses a card and reads the statement. Player identifies the statement as true, false or not in story, then attempts to toss the ball or beanbag into the correct basket or box. Player receives five points for stating the correct answer and five points if the ball or beanbag lands in the basket or box. If player does not give the correct answer, state the correct answer. The player may still earn five points by tossing ball or beanbag into the correct basket or box. Teams take turns. Question cards may be reused. Scorekeeper records each team's score on large sheet of paper or chalkboard.

Count Your Cards!

Materials Checklist
- [ ] 30 large index cards
- [ ] number cube
- [ ] pen

Preparation
On each index card, write a true or false statement about any Bible stories children have studied so far.

Procedure
Place cards facedown in five rows with six cards to a row. Divide group into two teams. Player from first team rolls number cube. He or she counts that number from the top left card across row to the right. Player turns over card (see sketch) and reads statement aloud.

Player's team identifies the statements as true or false. If correct response is given, team keeps the card. If incorrect response is given, player replaces the card facedown. (If the statement is false, team must correct the statement in order to gain the card.) Player from second team repeats process, counting from the card which was turned over (moving horizontally or vertically). Play continues in this manner. When all cards have been collected or time is up, team with most cards wins the game.

Luke preached to the crowd on Pentecost.

Hit or Miss Game

Materials Checklist

☐ large sheet of paper and felt pen

☐ blindfold

☐ masking tape

Preparation

Write on the paper 10-15 words that were mentioned in the session's Bible story. Add some words that have nothing at all to do with the story. (See sketch.) Attach paper to wall or bulletin board at children's eye level.

Procedure

Blindfold a volunteer. At a distance of about 5 feet (1.5 m) turn volunteer around three times and direct him or her toward the paper. Volunteer touches paper with index finger. Remove blindfold. If volunteer "hits" a word by touching it, he or she tells if the word belongs in the Bible story. If the word belongs, volunteer (or classmate chosen by volunteer) uses the word in a sentence telling information from the Bible story. Repeat process with additional volunteers until all words have been used.

Cornelius   prison   dream   dinner
tree   Joppa   Caesarea   soldiers   animals
Gentile   Peter
unclean   bread   sheet   Jewish
angel   salvation   robbers

That's the Way It Was

Materials Checklist

- [ ] slips of paper
- [ ] pen
- [ ] chair for each child except one

Preparation

For each child, except one, choose a word that is repeated several times in the lesson's Bible story. Write the words on slips of paper—one word on each slip. Place chairs in a circle.

Procedure

Children sit on chairs. One child stands in the middle of the circle. Give one slip of paper to each seated child. Read or tell the Bible story with expression. Each time you say a word that is on a slip of paper, the child holding that slip must stand, turn around and sit down again in the same chair. Meanwhile, the player in the middle tries to sit on the chair before the child sits down. If the player in the middle succeeds, the child now without a seat becomes the player in the middle and gives his or her slip to the child now seated. Continue telling the story at a pace that is comfortable for your students.

Variation

For an added challenge, insert the phrase "That's the way it was!" at various times during the story. Whenever you say this phrase, all children must stand and find a new seat. The player in the middle can use this opportunity to find a seat. The child left without a seat after the scramble will be the player in the middle as you continue to read the story.

Concentration

Materials Checklist
- [ ] tagboard
- [ ] felt pen
- [ ] scissors

Preparation
Cut tagboard into 16 4-inch (10-cm) squares. With felt pen, number the squares 1 through 16. On the opposite side of cards, write eight sentences from the lesson's Bible story—half a sentence on each card (see sketch). Make one set of game cards for every four children.

Procedure
Lay cards, with numbered sides up, on floor or table. Children take turns turning over two cards at a time. If the two cards chosen make a complete statement, the child may keep the cards and take another turn. When all cards have been matched, have children read the sentences in the correct order to review the Bible story.

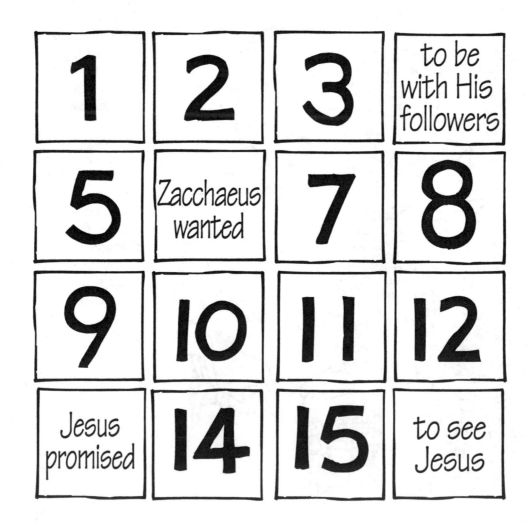

Question Cube

Materials Checklist

- ☐ square-shaped box (6×6 inches [15×15 cm] or larger)
- ☐ felt pens
- ☐ butcher paper
- ☐ scissors
- ☐ chalkboard and chalk
- ☐ tape
- ☐ glue

Preparation

If necessary, cover box with butcher paper. On the sides of the box, letter each of the following words—a different word on each side: "Who?," "What?," "When?," "Where?," "Why?," "Free points!"

Procedure

Divide class into two teams. Play begins as a volunteer from Team A rolls the question cube. If the word "Why?" lands faceup the volunteer must use the word "Why?" in a question he or she makes up after the day's Bible story. For example, "Why did the son want to leave his father's home?"

Players on Team B who want to answer the question stand up quickly. The first player who stands may answer for his or her team. For each correct answer, the team is given ten points. Keep score on a chalkboard. When the game is over say, **You remembered a lot of facts from our story today! What do you think is the most important thing God wants us to remember?**

If your students have difficulty coming up with questions, you may want to have a list of questions prepared that can be read by the students.

Friendly Feud Quiz Game

Materials Checklist

- ☐ small index cards (one for each child)
- ☐ table
- ☐ a chair for each child
- ☐ game bell
- ☐ chalkboard and chalk for keeping score

Preparation

On index cards, letter questions about recent lessons. Questions can include Bible story review, personal life application and Bible memory verse review.

Procedure

Divide class into two teams. Have them sit in rows or chairs facing each other. Place the game bell on a table between the two rows.

Have the first person from each team come to the table. Have each contestant stand with one hand on the table and one hand behind his or her back. Read aloud the question on the first card. The first person to ring the bell may answer the question for ten points. If he or she is wrong, the other contestant may answer it, winning five points for his or her team. If neither contestant gets the answer, put the question at the bottom of the pile to be asked later. Repeat procedure until all players have had several turns. Keep score on the chalkboard. When game is over ask, **If we could remember only one thing from today's lesson, what do you think God would want it to be?**

Middler/Bible Story Review

Toss 'n Tell

Materials Checklist

- [ ] large sheet of newsprint
- [ ] felt pens
- [ ] measuring stick
- [ ] several bean bags

Preparation

Divide paper into nine sections using pen and measuring stick (see sketch). Letter the words Who, What, When, Where and Why and four *Xs* on paper as in sketch.

Procedure

Place paper on floor in open area of room. Children stand at least four feet (1.2 m) from paper. Each child takes a turn to toss a bean bag onto the paper. Child then reviews the Bible story by answering the question on which the bean bag landed. (Example: Who? Abraham and Sarah; What? God promised Abraham a child; When? In Old Testament times; Where? in the Promised Land—Canaan; Why? Because God wanted to make a great nation out of Abraham's descendants. Children may think of many answers to the same questions.)

If the bean bag lands on an *X*, the child tosses the bean bag again—until the bean bag lands on a question.

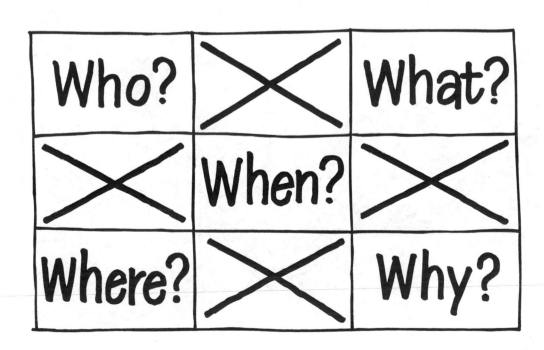

Traffic Jam

Materials Checklist

- [ ] Bible
- [ ] 50 large index cards
- [ ] four small pictures or stickers showing cars and trucks
- [ ] glue
- [ ] felt pen
- [ ] butcher paper or chalkboard and chalk

Preparation

Letter Bible Memory verse on chalkboard or paper. Letter the alphabet on index cards—one letter on each card. (Omit the letters *Q*, *X* and *Z*.) Make two sets of alphabet cards. Glue car and truck pictures to four extra index cards. Place two in each set.

Procedure

Divide the class into two teams. Give each team a set of cards to be divided as evenly as possible among team members. Teacher calls out first word of Bible Memory verse. The players holding the letters in the word arrange themselves to correctly spell out word. If a letter is used more than once in a word, player holding card with picture may substitute it for duplicate letter. When team members think they are in the correct order, they yell "Traffic Jam!" The other team must freeze in position. If the word is spelled correctly, then the team gets one point, and game continues on to next word of memory verse. When all words have been spelled, team with the most points wins. For difficult or new words, ask a volunteer to tell the meaning of the word. Ask, **Now that we know what each word means, what does this verse say to you? When might it help you to remember this verse?** (Volunteers answer.)

Glove Pass

Materials Checklist

- [ ] Bible
- [ ] cassette tape of children's songs
- [ ] index cards
- [ ] felt pens
- [ ] paper bag
- [ ] cassette
- [ ] one gardening glove

Preparation

Letter each word of a Bible memory verse on a separate index card.

Procedure

Place index cards in order on the floor and read verse aloud with children. Repeat several times. Then place cards in a paper bag. Children form a circle. While you play music on cassette player, children pass a gardening glove from player to player. To pass the glove, each player must put it on his or her neighbor's hand, then player takes it off and puts it on the next player. When you stop the music, player wearing the glove chooses a card from the bag. Player reads the word aloud and tries to complete the verse, beginning with that word.

Listen Up!

Materials Checklist

☐ Bible

☐ large index cards

☐ felt pen

Preparation

On index cards, letter the words and reference of the session's Bible Memory verse—one word on each card. Make two sets of cards.

Procedure

Arrange one set of Bible Memory verse cards in order on the floor. Children gather around cards and read verse aloud. Read verse with children several times so they become very familiar with it. Then divide class into two teams. Teams line up as in sketch. Shuffle both sets of verse cards together and spread all cards facedown on the floor as in sketch.

Assign each child a number. Use the same set of numbers for each team. (*Optional:* Instead of assigning numbers to children, assign each child the name of an animal such as squirrel, blue jay, chipmunk, rabbit, mouse, deer, etc.) To begin play, call out any one of the numbers you have assigned to children. Each of the two children with this number quickly chooses any one of the cards on the floor and brings it to his or her team. Repeat process. As children bring cards to their teams, team members try to place the cards in order. If a child brings a duplicate card, player who is called next returns card to pile before choosing a new card. Team which first places all cards in order wins.

1

2

3

4

5

5

4

3

2

1

index cards

Short Order Verse

Materials Checklist

- [ ] Bible
- [ ] large index cards
- [ ] felt pen

Preparation

Letter a Bible memory verse on index cards—one word on each card. Make two sets of cards. Mix up the cards within each set.

Procedure

Divide class into two teams. Each team sits or stands together. Distribute one set of cards among the players of each team. To begin play, read a phrase (four to six words) from Bible memory verse. Team members holding cards with the words of the phrase quickly move to the front of the room and arrange themselves in order (see sketch). When cards are in order, team members not holding cards read the phrase aloud. The team which completes this procedure first is the winner of that round. After both teams have read phrase aloud, discuss phrase by asking questions such as, **How would you say this phrase in simpler words? What instruction is given in this phrase?** Repeat game using different Bible Memory verse phrases each time. (*Optional:* Increase the difficulty of the game by using longer phrases.)

Three in a Row

Materials Checklist

- [ ] Bible
- [ ] construction paper in three colors
- [ ] large square of paper
- [ ] felt pen
- [ ] measuring stick
- [ ] scissors
- [ ] small paper bag

Preparation

Draw game board on large sheet of paper as shown in sketch. To make markers, cut six triangles from one color of construction paper, six circles from another color and six squares from a third color. Cut markers so that each will fit in a square on the game board. Put a triangle, a circle and a square in paper bag.

Procedure

Divide group into three teams. Give each team a set of five matching markers. To begin play, have a teacher or a child choose a marker from bag. Team with matching marker plays first. (Return marker to bag.) Teacher reads a Bible memory verse, leaving out a key word. If a team can tell the missing word, a volunteer from the team places a marker on any square of the game board. If they cannot tell the missing word, no marker is placed. Teacher or child chooses second marker from the bag and process is repeated using another memory verse. Teams continue taking turns until one team has placed three markers in a row. During the game, discuss verses by asking appropriate questions such as, **What does this verse tell you about God? What is one way you can obey this verse? Who in today's Bible story obeyed this verse?**

Build a Verse

Materials Checklist

- [ ] Bible
- [ ] chalkboard and chalk or large sheet of paper and felt pen

Preparation

None.

Procedure

Determine which word is in approximately the middle of a Bible memory verse children have memorized. Letter that word in center of chalkboard or large sheet of paper. Volunteer tells the word which comes before or after that word, then writes that word in the correct position. Continue building the verse by asking volunteers to write the appropriate "before" or "after" words. When Bible Memory verse is complete, read verse together. Ask questions such as, **When is a time you might need to remember this verse? How would you explain this verse to a friend?**

Group Effort

Materials Checklist

☐ large sheet of paper
☐ felt pens

Preparation

Letter Bible memory verse on sheet of paper. Divide verse into three or four sections by lettering each section with a different color felt pen.

Procedure

Divide class into three or four groups. Assign each group a section (color) of the Bible memory verse. Beginning slowly, point to groups one at a time to have them stand and recite their section of the verse. Repeat several times, increasing speed. Finally, take the sheet of paper away.

Variation

Have children do an action illustrating their section of the verse while saying it.

Mixed-Up Memory Verse

Materials Checklist
- [ ] two game bells

Preparation
None.

Procedure
Divide group into two teams. Each team stands or sits together around a game bell. Using a Bible memory verse the children have learned, the teacher slowly recites it, making several mistakes (either adding, deleting or substituting words). Each time the teacher makes a mistake, teams compete to ring the bell first. If the child who rings the bell first can correct the mistake, his or her team receives a point. If a child rings the bell when a mistake has *not* been made, his or her team loses a point. Repeat procedure several times for each verse the class has learned, making different mistakes each time.

(*Optional:* Teacher tells a short version of the lesson's Bible story, making mistakes which the children correct.)

Lord's Prayer Pass

Materials Checklist

- [ ] 52 small index cards
- [ ] felt pens
- [ ] large sheet of poster board

Preparation

Letter each of the following words on four index cards—one word to a card (as in sketch): "Father," "heaven," "Hallowed," "name," "kingdom," "will," "earth," "bread," "forgive, debts," "lead," "temptation," "deliver."

Procedure

Have children sit in a circle around a table or on the floor. Letter the words to the Lord's Prayer on a chalkboard or poster board. Read it aloud together with the children. One child mixes up the cards and distributes four to each player, setting remaining cards facedown in a pile. Players hold cards in one hand so they can easily see their own cards.

Each player will be trying to win the round by collecting four matching cards. Play begins as the distributor takes the top card from the facedown pile, and decides to keep it or pass it on facedown to the next person. If the distributor keeps the card he or she must take one of the four cards from his or her hand and pass it to the next person. The next person picks up the card and decides to keep it or to pass it. Meanwhile, the distributor continues to quickly pick up cards, keeping them or passing them on. At no time should a player have more than four cards in his or her hand. Passing continues until a player gets four alike and shouts out "Stop passing!" Play stops and other players count to ten in a whisper. While the players are counting, the player with four alike recites the phrase from the Lord's Prayer which contains the word in his or her hand. For example, if the word is "kingdom," he or she would say, "Thy kingdom come. Thy will be done on earth, as it is in heaven." If the phrase is recited correctly and before the players stop counting, the player may keep the four cards. Remaining cards are then mixed again and passed out for another round of play. The player with the most cards at the end of the game is the winner.

Memory Verse Freeze Tag

Materials Checklist

☐ several index cards with the day's Bible Memory verse lettered on them

Preparation

None.

Procedure

Prepare the children to succeed in the game by reviewing the Bible memory verse. Ask, **Why is it good to know Bible verses from memory? When might this verse help you?** Begin the game by establishing room or play area boundaries beyond which the children may not go. Choose a child to be "It." If tagged, the tagged child must freeze until the teacher comes by and the child is able to repeat the day's Bible memory verse. If the child is unable to say the verse, he or she may be given a copy of the verse to study while "frozen." After successfully saying the verse, the child may run freely again. At any point, teacher may yell, "Everybody freeze!" All children stop where they are, including "It." Teacher selects new "It" and then proceeds to unfreeze others by having them repeat the Bible memory verse.

Bible Balloon Bop

Materials Checklist
☐ several inflated balloons

Preparation
None.

Procedure
Review the Bible memory verse with the children. Ask, **Why do you think God put this verse in the Bible? In what way is this verse helpful to you?** Have class stand in a circle or on opposite sides of a line as in volleyball. A balloon is set in motion and bopped around the circle or back and forth across the line. The first player to hit the balloon says the first word of the Bible memory verse. The second player to hit the balloon says the second word and so on. If the balloon hits the ground, the opposite team wins a point. If a player cannot say his or her word, the opposite team wins a point. To vary the game, players can say one, two or three words of the verse at a time.

Chip Flip

Materials Checklist

- [ ] felt pens
- [ ] 12×12-inch (30×30-cm) piece of poster board
- [ ] pencil
- [ ] compass
- [ ] 8 small plastic chips (similar to those used in Tiddly Winks)

Preparation

Using pencil and compass, draw six concentric circles one inch (2.5 cm) apart on poster board (see sketch). Use felt pens to trace each circle a different color. Then, letter words of the Bible memory verse in circles, using different colors.

Procedure

Place game board on table or bare floor. Give each player two chips. First player places one chip on surface beside the game board and uses the other chip to "flip" it onto the target (as in a game of Tiddly Winks). Players take turns trying to land on the phrases in the correct order. For instance, player aims for "A wise man" first. After landing on that phrase, player tries for "will hear," etc. As player lands on each correct phrase, he or she may mark it with a removable sticker, self-adhesive note paper or penciled initials. Game continues until one player has completed the entire verse.

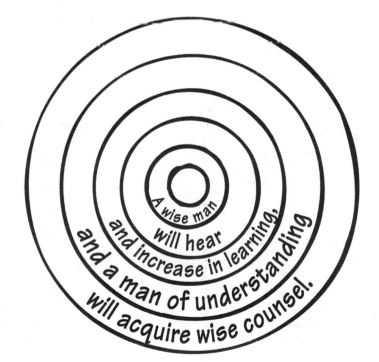

The Line-Up

Materials Checklist

☐ Bible

☐ large adhesive-backed labels

☐ fine-tip felt pen

Preparation

Divide the Bible memory verse into five or six sections. Letter each section of the verse on a separate label (see sketch).

Procedure

Read or ask a child to read or recite the Bible memory verse. Then adhere labels to the backs of five or six children. Don't let them see the lettering on their labels. Make sure there are a few children without labels. Children with labels change places several times to make sure their order is mixed up. Instruct the children without labels to verbally "arrange" those with labels into the correct order to form the verse. (Example: Child says, "Jeremy, stand to the right of Amber." "Now Lisa, move to the left of Amber.")

And we know	that all things	work together
for good	to them	that love God.

Bible Skullies

Materials Checklist

- [ ] Bible
- [ ] chalk
- [ ] soda bottle cap
- [ ] clay or play dough
- [ ] measuring stick

Preparation

On a paved area outdoors, use chalk to draw a 5-foot (1.5-m) square court as shown in sketch. Letter the words of memory verse and numbers in squares as shown. Make a game piece, called a "loady," by filling a soda bottle cap with clay or play dough and allowing it to harden.

Procedure

Read verse aloud with children. Repeat several times. Ask, **What does this verse tell us to do?** (Students respond.) **What is another word for ("honor")? To help us remember the words of our verse, we're going to play a street game called "Skullies."**

First player kneels behind outer line of court by square one and places loady on the ground outside of court. Player then recites first word of verse and tries to flick loady, smooth side down, into first square. If player succeeds, he or she may proceed to flick loady to second square and recite first two words of verse. If player misses, second player resumes where he or she left off, first saying words recited thus far. Players may kneel to flick loady at any point outside of court.

Continue process until entire verse has been recited. Repeat as time allows. (*Optional:* If loady is flicked outside of court, the next player must start at the beginning.)

Variation: Divide class into two teams. Players gain points each time loady lands in correct square.

Court diagram

5'

player ✗

Honor 1		your 8	the 6		your mother, 4
God 9		Deuteronomy 5:16 13			you. 12
com-manded 11					has 10
and 3		as 5	Lord 7		your father 2

5'

Verse Under Construction

Materials Checklist

- [ ] Bible
- [ ] two large toy dump trucks
- [ ] outdoor sandbox or plastic wading pool filled with sand
- [ ] scissors
- [ ] poster board (two colors)
- [ ] chalk and chalkboard or poster board and felt pen
- [ ] colored chalk or masking tape
- [ ] measuring stick

Preparation

Letter the words of memory verse on poster board. Cut into puzzle pieces—one piece for every two children (see sketch).

Make a matching set with a different color of poster board. Bury puzzle pieces in sandbox. Letter words of verse on chalkboard or poster board.

Use chalk or tape to mark a starting line 20 feet (6 m) from the sandbox. Mark two roads on the floor from starting line to the sandbox (see sketch).

Procedure

Read verse aloud with children. Repeat several times.

Divide class into two even teams. Teams line up behind starting line. First child on each team pushes truck along the road to the sandbox. Player then looks for a puzzle piece in his or her team's color, places the puzzle piece inside the truck and pushes truck back to the starting line following the same road. Second child on each team then takes his or her turn to retrieve a second puzzle piece. Game continues until all the puzzle pieces have been assembled and team recites verse.

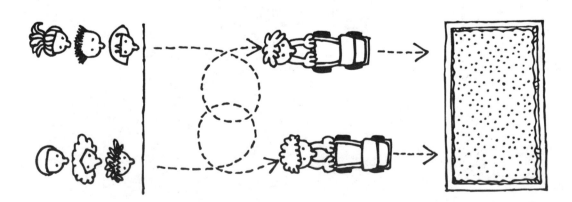

"Bear with each other and forgive whatever grievances you may have against one another. Forgive as the Lord forgave you." Colossians 3:13

Hula Hoop Hoopla

Materials Checklist

- [ ] Bible
- [ ] hula hoops—one for every five to six children
- [ ] chalk or construction paper
- [ ] masking tape and felt pen

Preparation

Letter the words of memory verse on five sheets of construction paper—one phrase on each card (sketch a). Tape cards in various locations around the room. (If playing outside, use chalk to letter each phrase on the ground in five different places within close proximity.)

Procedure

Read verse together. Then ask, **What does this verse mean?**

Divide class into teams of five or six children. Teams line up behind a designated point. First child from each team holds a hula hoop around his or her waist. When teacher recites first phrase of verse, first child on each team runs to corresponding location. Second child from each team then runs to first child and gets inside hula hoop. The pair then runs to next location as teacher recites second phrase of verse. One more child is added inside hula hoop each time a phrase of the verse is completed (sketch b). Play continues until all team members are inside hula hoops and memory verse has been recited several times. (*Optional:* Teams compete one at a time to see which team can run through the verse the fastest.)

a.

b.

Jump-a-Jingle

Materials Checklist

- ☐ Bible
- ☐ chalkboard and chalk or poster board and felt pen
- ☐ a jump rope for every four or five children

Preparation

Letter memory verse on chalkboard or poster board as shown in sketch.

Procedure

Using rhythm similar to the one shown, read verse aloud with children. Repeat several times.

Divide class into teams of four or five children. Allow children time to choose which team members will jump and which two will twirl the rope. Teams jump rope as they recite memory verse in rhythm. Teams compete by keeping track of how many times the verse is recited before missing.

Variation

For easier jump roping, players may jump individually or teams may simply swing rope back and forth.

Every-one should be
     1   2   3   4
quick to listen, slow to speak,
   5   6   7   8
and slow to become an-gry.
      9   10   11   12
James 1:19

Special Parts

Materials Checklist

- [ ] Bible
- [ ] chalk
- [ ] poster board
- [ ] felt pen
- [ ] crushed soda can

Preparation

Use chalk to draw four concentric circles on the ground (see sketch). Draw three pie cuts from the central circle to the outer circle. Letter the following body parts as shown in sketch: arms, legs, body, hands, feet, mouth, eyes, ears, nose and head. Mark a throwing line 4 feet (1.2 m) from outer circle.

On poster board, draw a blank line for each letter of the memory verse. (If time is limited, draw blank lines for only a portion of the verse.)

Procedure

Children line up behind throwing line. Children take turns tossing crushed can (token) into circle and guessing letters to complete Bible memory verse. Each time a child guesses correctly, write the letter on the correct line(s). Using chalk, child then draws on the ground the body part that his or her token has landed on. If a child guesses a letter incorrectly, write the incorrect letter off to the side.

The object of the game is for children to guess the Bible memory verse before completing the figure with all body parts. If the token lands outside of circles, player tosses token again. If token lands on a body part that has already been drawn, no body parts are drawn.

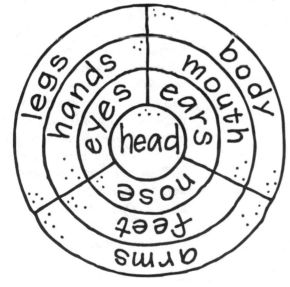

How great is the love the Father has lavished on us,

th_t _e sho____

_e ____ _e_ the

_h_____e_ o_

_o_. 1 John 3:1   kmj

Grape Suckers

Materials Checklist

- [ ] permanent felt pen
- [ ] 10 disposable cups
- [ ] plastic drinking straw for each student
- [ ] cluster of grapes with part of vine or long stem attached
- [ ] stopwatch

Preparation

Letter the words of memory verse on cups as shown.

Procedure

Display cups on a table and read the verse aloud several times with children. Ask, **What does this verse tell us to do?** (Students respond.) Distribute a straw and several grapes to each child. Divide class into two or more teams of 10 players or less. Mix up order of cups. Teams line up across the room from table. Start stopwatch as the first player on team one holds a grape by sucking through straw. Player runs to table, drops grape in the cup with the first word of verse and then moves the cup to the correct position on the table. Second player then sucks up a grape, runs to table, drops grape into cup with second word of verse and moves cup into correct position. Continue until all words of verse are in correct order. Stop the watch and record time. Repeat process with second, then third team. Repeat entire game as time allows. (*Optional:* Make two or three sets of cups and have teams race simultaneously.)

etc.

The Orange Bowl

Materials Checklist

- [ ] Bible
- [ ] two oranges
- [ ] 10 empty milk cartons
- [ ] 10 index cards
- [ ] felt pen
- [ ] masking tape

Preparation

Letter the words of memory verse on five index cards (see sketch). Tape to five milk cartons. Make a matching set. Hide the oranges somewhere in your classroom. Use tape to make two triangles on the floor. Arrange the milk cartons in V-shapes like bowling pins. Place strips of tape across the room from the milk cartons. Children stand behind strips when they bowl.

Procedure

Read verse aloud with children. Repeat several times.

Teams line up behind line of tape. A teacher or helper stands beside each team. First child on each team recites verse to teacher and rolls orange, trying to knock over milk cartons. He or she then places milk cartons back in order. Second child on each team then recites verse and takes a turn at bowling. Repeat until all children have had a turn.

Potato Catch

Materials Checklist

- [ ] chalkboard and chalk or butcher paper and felt pen
- [ ] masking tape
- [ ] two burlap potato sacks or paper bags

For each child—

- [ ] one small potato

Preparation

Letter the words of memory verse on the chalkboard or butcher paper. Place two strips of masking tape on the floor, approximately 4 yards (3.6 m) apart.

Procedure

Read verse aloud with children. Repeat several times. Divide class into two teams. Both teams line up behind one line of masking tape. Give each player a potato. First member of each team stands on opposite strip of tape and holds a potato sack (see sketch). At your signal, second member of each team recites verse, then turns around and tosses potato through his or her legs to player holding sack. Players holding sacks can move around to try to catch potatoes in sacks. Game continues until all players have recited verse and tossed a potato into sack. Repeat game as time allows.

Middler/Bible Memory Verse Review

Love Note Scrolls

Materials Checklist

- [ ] Bible
- [ ] large sheet of newsprint
- [ ] red and black felt markers
- [ ] scissors
- [ ] yarn
- [ ] masking tape

Preparation

Draw a large red heart on newsprint and cut it out. Use black marker to letter the Bible memory verse onto the newsprint heart (sketch a). Cut the newsprint heart into eight pieces. Roll each piece into a scroll and tie with yarn (sketch b). Hide scrolls around room or outdoor area.

Procedure

Ask, **Have you ever written or received a letter?** After responses, ask, **Why do people write letters?** Children respond. Hold up a Bible and say, **The Bible is like a letter God has sent to us. Now the Bible is in the form of a book, but when it was first written thousands of years ago, it was written on scrolls.** Children search for scrolls. When all eight have been found, children put pieces together to form heart, then tape pieces to the floor. Read verse aloud with children.

a.
"The plans of the Lord stand firm forever, the purposes of his heart through all generations."
Psalm 33:11

b.

Creation Mix-Up

Materials Checklist

- ☐ Bible
- ☐ index cards
- ☐ felt pen
- ☐ masking tape
- ☐ butcher paper

Preparation

Letter one word of the Bible memory verse on each index card (sketch a). On opposite sides, letter the names of things God created. Number the cards in order (sketch b). On butcher paper, write numbers, leaving space for cards above numbers (sketch c). Tape paper to wall.

Procedure

Tape a card onto the back of each child. (Teacher holds onto any extra cards.) Explain that each child has the name of one of God's creations on his or her back. Children try to guess what names they have on their backs by asking yes or no questions of other children in the room (i.e., "Is it an animal? Does it have four legs?" Or, "Is it a plant? Is it bigger than a toaster? Is it a tree?"). After child has guessed correctly, he or she takes off the card and tapes it to the corresponding numbered place on the butcher paper. (Teacher tapes extra cards in appropriate places.) When all of the cards have been put in their proper places, children read the verse aloud in unison. Ask, **What do you learn about God from this verse?** (Children answer.)

a.

| Know | that | the |

b.

| ¹ star | ² snake | ³ cat |

c.

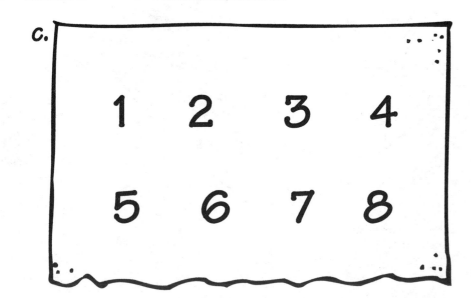

Musical Praise

Materials Checklist

- [ ] Bible
- [ ] children's music cassette
- [ ] one chair for each child
- [ ] masking tape
- [ ] bright piece of paper or fabric
- [ ] cassette player
- [ ] newsprint and felt pen or chalkboard and chalk
- [ ] 8-12 small index cards

Preparation

Letter the Bible memory verse on chalkboard or newsprint and display in visible location. Place chairs in a large circle, facing inward. Tape a bright piece of paper or fabric to one chair.

Procedure

As you play music, children walk around circle of chairs. When music stops, each child sits in a chair. The child sitting in the marked chair stands up and tapes an index card over any part of the verse, horizontally or vertically (see sketch). The class then recites the verse. Continue playing game until all words are covered and children are able to say the entire verse from memory.

Praise the ☐
How good it is to sing
praises to our ☐
how pleasant and
☐ to praise ☐
Psalm 147:1

Memory Verse Message

Materials Checklist

- [ ] Bible
- [ ] chalkboard and chalk or sheet of butcher paper
- [ ] felt pen and tape or tacks

Preparation

On sheet of butcher paper or chalkboard, letter the first part of the Bible memory verse and draw a blank line for each letter of the remainder of the verse (see sketch). Attach paper to wall.

Procedure

Children take turns guessing letters that might complete the missing words of the memory verse. Each time a child guesses correctly, write the letter on the correct line (or lines). Each time a child guesses incorrectly, write the incorrect letter off to the side and draw a part of a person (sketch b). If you complete the drawing before the children complete the verse, you win the game! If the children complete the verse before you complete the person, they win! (Gauge how much of the person to draw after each miss so that children really do win!)

a.

For to us a child is born, to us a son is given...
And he will be called _ _ _ _ _ _ _ _ _
_ _ _ _ _ _ _ _ _, _ _ _ _ _ _
_ _ _ , _ _ _ _ _ _ _ _ _
_ _ _ _ _ _ _ , _ _ _ _ _
_ _ _ _ _ _ _. Isaiah 9:6

b.

Illustrated Verse

Materials Checklist
- [ ] Bible
- [ ] three large sheets of butcher paper
- [ ] tempera paints and paint-brushes
- [ ] felt pens

Preparation
Letter a portion of the Bible memory verse across the top of each sheet of paper (see sketch). If your group has nine or more students, prepare an extra set of papers.

Procedure
Read verse aloud with children. Divide class into three groups. Groups should have two or three members each. (For a larger class, divide into six groups.) Assign each group to illustrate a portion of the verse using paints or felt pens. When groups are finished, display papers in your classroom. Read verse aloud again.

"And if I go and prepare a place for you,

I will come back

and take you to be with me that you also may be where I am." John 14:3

Mountain Verse Trail

Materials Checklist

- ☐ Bible
- ☐ construction paper
- ☐ scissors
- ☐ felt marker
- ☐ masking tape

Preparation

Trace around your feet on construction paper and cut out footprints—two for each word in the memory verse. Letter each word from the Bible memory verse on two footprints, making two sets of footprints lettered with the verse. Tape footprints to floor in order, making two separate verse trails (see sketch).
(*Optional:* Have children tape footprints to floor.)

Procedure

Divide class into two teams. Each team lines up behind a verse trail. From your Bible, read the Bible memory verse to children. All children recite verse together as team members take turns stepping on footprints. With each repeat, remove one footprint from each path, until last player can follow route without reference to any footprints.

Middler/Bible Memory Verse Review

Think Fast!

Materials Checklist

- [ ] Bible
- [ ] large piece of paper
- [ ] felt pen and masking tape or chalkboard and chalk
- [ ] rubber or sponge ball

Preparation

Letter memory verse on paper or chalkboard.

Procedure

Children sit in a circle. Read verse several times with children. Begin game by throwing ball to one child who must say the first word of the verse. Child then throws the ball to any other child who must say the second word of the verse. Continue until all words of the verse have been said. When children are very familiar with the verse, take down or erase verse and play the game saying the words from memory.

Connect-a-Verse Game

Materials Checklist

- ☐ Bibles
- ☐ lightweight cardboard or poster board
- ☐ pen
- ☐ scissors
- ☐ ruler
- ☐ stapler
- ☐ string
- ☐ large sheet of paper or chalkboard and chalk

Preparation

Cut cardboard or poster board into a 4x8-inch (10x20-cm) rectangle. Cut notches along opposite edges as in sketch. Attach a 4-foot (1.2-m) length of string and letter the Bible memory verse as shown in sketch. Repeat procedure to make a connect-a-verse game for every 2-3 children. Letter Bible memory verse on large sheet of paper or chalkboard.

Procedure

Referring to Bible memory verse lettered on paper or chalkboard, children take turns using string to connect the words of the verse in order. (Warn children that several of the words do not belong in the verse.) When children have had a turn to connect the words, they read verse in unison.

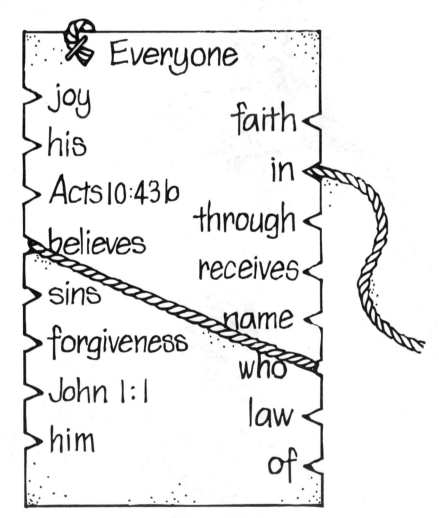

Bible Verse Quilt

Materials Checklist

- ☐ Bible
- ☐ large sheet of paper
- ☐ felt pen
- ☐ poster board or construction paper
- ☐ scissors
- ☐ masking tape

Preparation

Letter Bible memory verse on a large sheet of paper. Hang in visible location. Also letter Bible memory verse on a sheet of poster board. Cut apart poster board as shown in sketch to make a set of shapes. Make one set for each group of five or six children.

Procedure

Give a set of shapes to each group of five or six children. Children take turns choosing shapes until all have been chosen. Then say, **The person whose birthday is closest to today will be the first player in your group.** He or she places a shape on the table or floor. Then children work together to determine whose shape should be added next. Children continue adding shapes until the Bible verse is complete. After completing verse, read it together.

Command them to do good, to be rich in good deeds, and to be generous and willing to share. 1 Timothy 6:18

Circle Words

Materials Checklist

- ☐ Bible
- ☐ large sheet of paper and felt pen or chalkboard and chalk
- ☐ pencils
- ☐ drawing paper

Preparation

Letter large paper or chalkboard as shown in sketch.

Procedure

Give each child drawing paper and pencil. Say, **Try to discover the words of our Bible memory verse. The letters in each circle make a word. The letters are written in order. However, the position of the first letter in the word is different in each circle.** Children may work together in pairs or trios if they wish. Give help as needed. When children have written the verse on paper, read the verse together. If time permits, children find and read verse in Bibles.

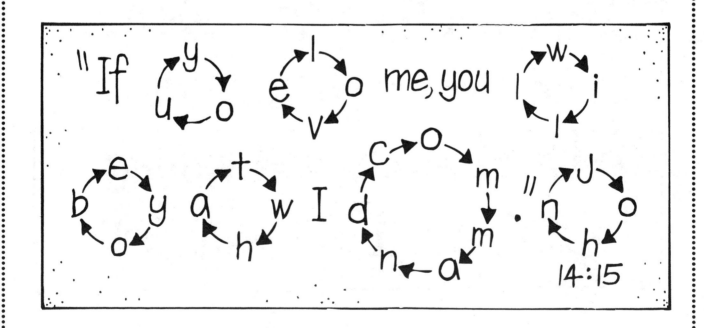

Building Block
Bible Verse

Materials Checklist

☐ Bibles

☐ wooden building blocks
(or construction paper pieces
approximately 2×4-inches
[5×10-cm])

☐ felt pen

☐ large sheet of paper or
chalkboard and chalk

Preparation

Letter Bible memory verse on blocks, one word on each block. Write the Scripture reference on the last block. (*Optional:* If wooden blocks are not available, letter verse and reference on construction paper rectangles.) Letter Bible memory verse on large sheet of paper or chalkboard.

Procedure

Read Bible memory verse with children. Ask children to arrange wooden or paper blocks in order. Read verse again. As time permits, children mix up blocks and arrange them in order to build a variety of shapes in which the verse can be read: square, triangle, rectangle, circle, pyramid.

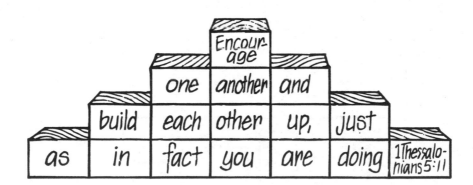

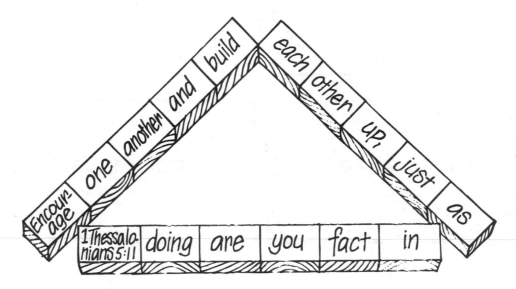

Hidden Bible Verse

Materials Checklist

- [ ] Bible
- [ ] construction paper
- [ ] felt pens
- [ ] scissors
- [ ] index cards
- [ ] pencils

Preparation

Cut out sections in one sheet of paper (sketch a).

Then place cut-out paper on top of another sheet of paper. Letter as shown in sketch b. After removing paper with cut-out windows, add additional letters as shown in sketch c. Repeat this process, lettering the remaining four-word segments of the Bible memory verse on three additional sheets of paper. (Use the same cut-out sheet for all phrases.) Prepare a set of these papers for each group of six to eight children.

Procedure

Show one set of the lettered papers. **Today's Bible memory verse is hidden on these papers. With your group, discover the words by placing the paper with cut-out sections on top of each lettered paper.** Demonstrate this instruction and then say, **One person in your group should write on a separate index card each phrase you discover. When you have discovered each phrase, put the three cards in order.** When groups have put the index cards in order, read verse aloud.

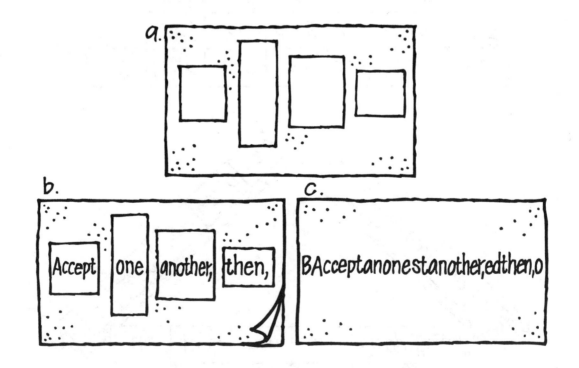

Balloon Surprise!

Materials Checklist

- [ ] balloons
- [ ] felt marker
- [ ] clothespins
- [ ] 6- to 8-foot (1.8 to 2.4-m) length of string

Preparation

Blow up a balloon for each word in Bible verse. Letter one word on each balloon, then deflate balloons. Tie string across front of bulletin board.

Procedure

Direct each child to blow up a balloon and hang it from string. Children then try to put the balloons in the correct order. After reading the verse aloud in unison, let children take turns popping a balloon, then having rest of group say verse correctly. Continue until all balloons are popped and complete verse can be said.

Verse Number Puzzle

Materials Checklist

- ☐ Bible
- ☐ two large sheets of paper and felt pen or chalk and chalkboard

Preparation

Letter papers or chalkboard with encoded verse and number grid as in sketches.

Procedure

Show children paper or chalkboard lettered with encoded verse. Say, **Each group of numbers under a blank line represents a letter.** Show number grid. **To find each letter, trace the grid from number to number.** (Example: 143 will make an *L*.) **Where numbers are divided by a dash, do not connect them on the grid. We will fill in each missing letter to complete the verse.** Have volunteers take turns filling in letters. Read completed Bible memory verse together.

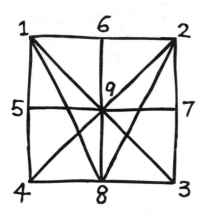

"GOD WANTS ALL M____ ____ .
      2143-57 4132

TO BE ____ A ____ ____ D
      215734   182   2143-57

AND TO COME TO A

K____ ____ W____ ____DGE
 4132 12341 143 2143-57

OF THE ____R ____ ____H."
        12-68   1432 1268

1 TIMOTHY 2:4

Secret Message Rebus

Materials Checklist

- [ ] construction paper
- [ ] scissors
- [ ] felt pens or pencils

Preparation

Draw a rebus of the memory verse (see sketch) on construction paper, one for every two children. (*Optional:* Draw rebus once and photocopy for each additional pair of children.) Cut each rebus into jigsaw pieces.

Procedure

Say, **A secret message has been cut apart. Your assignment is to put the pieces back together and figure out the message.** Divide the class into pairs. Give each pair a rebus puzzle to put together and guide children to decode the message. When the Bible memory verse has been decoded, recite the verse with the children.

Puzzle Put-Together

Materials Checklist

- ☐ Bible
- ☐ four different-colored sheets of construction paper
- ☐ felt pen
- ☐ scissors

Preparation

Cut each color of paper into a different geometric shape (circle, triangle, square, rectangle). Letter memory verse on shapes, one word or phrase on each shape (see sketch). Cut each shape into three or four pieces. (For large groups make several puzzle sets.)

Procedure

Distribute one or more puzzle pieces to each child. Say, **Find other people with puzzle pieces the same color as yours. Put your pieces together to form a word. Then put the words in order to discover an important message.**

Middler/Bible Memory Verse Review

Memory Challenge

Materials Checklist

- ☐ small index cards
- ☐ felt pens
- ☐ chalkboard and chalk
- ☐ newsprint

Preparation

Letter today's Bible memory verse on the chalkboard or newsprint. Letter the Bible memory verse on index cards, one word or short phrase on each card. Prepare enough sets of verse cards for several teams of children.

Procedure

Divide the class into teams, giving each team a set of cards. Say, **We are going to have a contest to see which team can arrange the words from our memory verse in the correct order first. You may refer to the verse on the board for help.** After each team has their cards arranged in the correct sequence, remove the verse from the board. Have the children mix the cards again and try to put them in the correct sequence from memory. If there is time, remove some cards from each team's set. Have a team member read the verse aloud to you with the rest of the team supplying the missing words or phrases from memory. Ask, **What does this verse say about God?**

Picture Perfect

Materials Checklist

- ☐ Bible
- ☐ felt pen
- ☐ glue
- ☐ ruler

For each group of three to four children—

- ☐ picture from magazine or comic section of the newspaper (approximately 8 1/2×11-inches [21.5×27.5-cm])
- ☐ one manila folder
- ☐ sheet of white construction paper

Preparation

Glue a magazine picture to a sheet of white paper. Allow to dry. Turn the sheet over and divide the white paper into eight equal sections. On each section, letter a phrase of the Bible memory verse (see sketch). Cut the sections apart and place them in a manila folder. Repeat procedure to make one puzzle for each group of three or four children in your class.

Procedure

Divide class into groups of three or four children. Give each group a puzzle. Instruct children to work together to put the Bible memory verse in order on one side of the open folder. When they think they have it right they can close the folder, turn the puzzle over and look at the picture. If the picture fits together correctly, the verse is also correct.

"The Son of God	has come and
has given us	understanding,
so that we	may know
him who is	true." I John 5:20

Who Is Our Refuge?

Materials Checklist

- [ ] felt pen
- [ ] chalk
- [ ] chalkboard
- [ ] 2×2-inch (5×5-cm) card

Preparation

Letter Bible memory verse on card and chalkboard.

Procedure

(Adapted from "Button, button, who's got the button?") Children stand in a circle and put their hands behind their backs. Teacher chooses one child to be "It" who stands aside. The teacher walks around the outside of the circle pretending to place the Bible memory verse card in the hands of each child, and actually places it into one child's hands along the way. "It" tries to figure out who has the card. He or she approaches a child and says, "Who is our refuge?" (Adapt question according to your verse.) If the child does not have the card he or she answers, "Keep searching," and "It" approaches another child. If the child does have the card, he or she will answer with the memory verse, "God is our refuge and strength, an ever present help in trouble." At this point the child with the card becomes "It." The former "It" goes around the circle and deposits the card in the hands of another child. Play continues until every child has had a chance to be "It."

Search n' Match

Materials Checklist

- [ ] small index cards
- [ ] felt pen
- [ ] scissors

Preparation

Prepare one card for every two children. Letter each card with one of the "Good News" statements below. Cut the cards so that half of the statement is on one half of the card and the second half of the statement is on the second half of the card.

Procedure

Distribute a half card to each child. Say, **Today you are going to share some good news with the class. However, each of you has only one half of the news. Your job is to find the person with the other half. When you have found your match, come back to the circle and sit next to that person.**

Jesus is / God's Son.

Jesus died / for my sins.

You can be a member / of God's family.

God can / forgive our sins.

God / answers prayers.

I can tell others / about Jesus.

God will / protect me.

Jesus promised / eternal life.

The Bible is / the Word of God.

Kick the Can Acrostic

Materials Checklist

- [ ] chalkboard and chalk or newsprint pads and felt pens
- [ ] masking tape

For every three to six students—

- [ ] one empty soda can

Preparation

On chalkboard or newsprint, vertically letter a key word from your lesson (see sketch)—once for each team of three to six children. Use masking tape to make starting line 20-30 feet (6-9 m) from chalkboard or newsprint.

Procedure

Divide class into teams of three to six children. Teams line up behind starting line. First player on each team kicks soda can to chalkboard or newsprint and fills in acrostic with a way to demonstrate the word (see sketch). Team members then kick the can back to second player on team. Team members take turns filling in acrostic. First team to complete acrostic wins. As time allows, repeat game with different words.

Forgive my sister.
T**A**lk about the problem.
M
I
sa**Y** I'm sorry.

Quick Answer

Materials Checklist

- [ ] Bible
- [ ] poster board
- [ ] felt pen
- [ ] a soft object (Nerf ball, plastic ball or beanbag) for each team
- [ ] watch or clock with a second hand
- [ ] tape or tacks

Preparation

Letter the fruit of the Spirit on poster board. Use tape or tacks to attach poster to wall.

Procedure

Divide class into teams of five or six students each. Each team sits in a circle on the floor. Review with children the definition of each fruit of the Spirit. Say, **To play this game you need to be prepared to say a way you can show each of the first five fruit of the Spirit in your life. For example, what are some ways you can show love to another person? How can you show that you have joy? Peace? When can you be patient? Kind?** Lead children in suggesting answers. At your signal the first player names a fruit of the Spirit and tosses the ball to another player. The player catching the ball must name a way he or she can demonstrate that fruit. The second player then names another fruit of the Spirit and tosses the ball to a third player. (All five fruits must be named before any can be repeated. Ways to show the fruit may not be repeated.) A teacher or helper is assigned to each team to count the fruit named. Round continues until time is called (approximately one minute). The object of the game is to see which team can name the most fruit of the Spirit during the time allotted. Repeat game as time allows. You may want to vary each game by allowing players to change teams.

Letter Stand-Up

Materials Checklist

☐ index cards

☐ felt pens

☐ pencil and paper for keeping score

Preparation

Write each of the following letters on a separate index card—*l, o, v, e, j, o, y, p, a, c, e, t, i, n, k, d, n, s, s.* Make two sets of cards. (*Optional:* Include additional letters to spell the words "goodness," "faithfulness," "gentleness" and "self-control.")

Procedure

Divide class into two teams and have them sit on the floor. Distribute one set of cards to the players on each team. (Team members will receive more than one card. Don't give one player two of the same letter.) To play the game, call out one fruit of the Spirit (love, joy, peace, patience, kindness). Players on each team who are holding letters in the word quickly stand up and arrange themselves in order to spell the word. The first team to complete the word scores a point. Bonus points may be scored by either or both teams if one of the players can name a way a person might demonstrate that characteristic at school (home, church, etc.). To help students, ask questions such as, **What is one way a person might show love at home? What is a reason a person might be joyful at Sunday School? How might a person show that he or she has peace? When could a person be patient? Kind?**

Winners' Circle

Materials Checklist

- ☐ Children's music cassette and cassette player
- ☐ an index card for each child
- ☐ felt pen
- ☐ masking tape

Optional—

- ☐ chalk

Preparation

Divide cards into three equal sets. Letter the words "share," "be kind," "forgive" and "be patient" (or other words related to your lesson) on one set of index cards—one word or phrase on each card. (If necessary, you may make duplicates.) Letter a location on each of the second set of cards (i.e., classroom, home, store, playground, bus, car, kitchen, bedroom, backyard, park, beach, swimming pool). Letter a person on each of the third set of cards (i.e., boy, girl, baby, mom, dad, grandma, neighbor, five-year-old child, teenager, teacher). Use masking tape to create three large circles, and various "rocks" on the floor (see sketch). Make one "rock" for each child. Make an *X* on three of the rocks as in sketch.

(*Optional:* If you are able to play this game outdoors on cement or asphalt surface, use chalk to draw circles and "rocks.")

Procedure

Divide class into three equal teams. Team one stands on "rocks" in outer circle. Team two stands on "rocks" in center circle and so on. Give each child in the outer circle an index card with a location lettered on it. Give each child in the middle circle an index card with a person lettered on it. Give each child in the inner circle an index card with a Bible word lettered on it. As cassette is played, children hop clockwise around circles from "rock" to "rock." When the music stops, children on the "rocks" marked *X* read the information on their cards. Then the first player to raise his or her hand may use all the information on the three cards to tell how a person might obey God. (For example, "Mom was patient when she had to wait in line at the store.") Player's team receives a point. The first team to earn five points is the winning circle.

Share

be kind   forgive

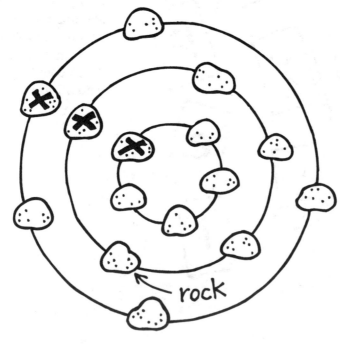

rock

The ABC Game

Materials Checklist

☐ large sheet of paper and felt pens or chalkboard and chalk

Preparation

Print letters of alphabet along left side of paper or chalkboard (sketch a). Assign a number value from 1-10 to each letter. Assign low numbers to commonly used letters such as *A* or *N*. Assign high numbers to letters such as *Q* or *Z*. Print each number value next to its assigned letter. Letter a separate piece of paper or chalkboard as in sketch b.

Procedure

Divide class into two to four teams. Teams take turns thinking of sentences or phrases describing specific ways to obey God. Children write sentences or phrases on the paper or chalkboard beside the appropriate letter of the alphabet (sketch c). Team receives the number score assigned to the letter they used. Teams do not have to suggest sentences in the order of the alphabet. Team with the highest score when time is called, or when no team can suggest additional sentences, is the winner. (*Optional:* All children work together to see how many points they can accumulate.)

a.

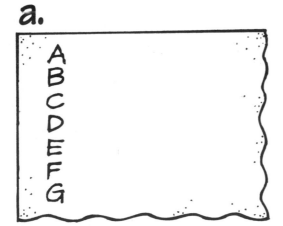

A
B
C
D
E
F
G

b.

Ways to Be Wise
- Make Peace
- Work Hard
- Serve Others
- Do Good
- Trust God

c.

A = 1 Avoiding an argument will help make peace.
B = 2
C = 3 Cleaning my room is a way I work hard.
D = 2
E = 4
F = 4
G = 5 God listens when I pray.

Mix and Match Pantomimes

Materials Checklist

- [ ] pencil
- [ ] small index cards
- [ ] bowl or small bag

Preparation

Think of words which describe principles discussed with children during their lessons. Plan enough words so that there is one letter for each child. Suggested words: "forgive," "pray," "generous," "share," "love," "obey," "help," "encourage." Write two or three letters of each word on separate index cards. Number all cards for a particular word with the same number (see sketch). Shuffle cards and place in bowl or bag.

Procedure

Each child chooses a card from bowl or bag. (Keep remaining cards.) Then say, **At my signal, get together with anyone whose number matches yours.** When groups have gathered, give any remaining cards to appropriate groups. **Now put your letters together to make a word. Keep your word secret. The word you discover will remind you of an action we have talked about during our lessons.** After groups have identified their words, allow time for each group to think of a way for one or more members of the group to silently dramatize the word. Groups take turns presenting pantomimes as children in other groups try to guess the word. After each word has been guessed, ask questions about the word such as, **When can you obey God? encourage others? When has someone forgiven you?**

What's the Number?

Materials Checklist

- [ ] large sheet of poster board
- [ ] construction paper
- [ ] scissors
- [ ] transparent tape
- [ ] felt pen
- [ ] writing paper

Preparation

On a sheet of paper, write nine questions about the lessons children have studied. These questions can be about Bible memory verse and/or personal life application. Questions must be able to be answered with one word. Letter the answer to each question twice on poster board (see sketch). Cut construction paper into 18 small rectangles and tape to poster board. Use felt pen to number flaps.

Procedure

Divide group into two teams and assign the order in which they will play. Read aloud the first question. Player from first team tries to guess the locations of the matching answers by calling out the number of two flaps on the game board. If the team succeeds in uncovering the correct answer-flaps, the flaps are removed and given to the team. If team locates only one or none of the correct answers, flaps are left in place and second team takes a turn. Teams take turns until flaps for the first question have been removed. Game continues until flaps have been removed for all questions.

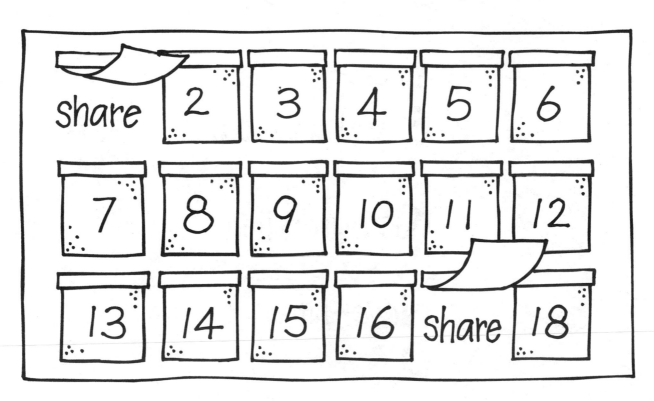

Acrostic Relay

Materials Checklist
☐ chalkboard and chalk or newsprint pads and felt pens
☐ kitchen timer

Preparation
On chalkboard or newsprint, vertically letter a Bible phrase about love (see sketch). Letter the same phrase on another section of chalkboard or another sheet of newsprint, so there is one acrostic for each team.

Procedure
Divide class into two teams. Set kitchen timer for five minutes. Team members take turns filling in acrostic with ways to show God's love. The winner is the team who has filled in the most ways to show God's love, when the timer rings.

Let my sister go first

Offer to help

V

Ob**E**y my parents

I

Say thank you.

Kiss grandma

G**I**ve a present

Never hit

D

Puppet Plays

Materials Checklist

- ☐ two puppets
- ☐ pencil
- ☐ small index cards
- ☐ small box

Preparation

On each card write a simple situation that can be acted out by two puppets (see sketch). The situations should be open-ended, allowing children to choose responses that will apply the Bible truth learned to recent lessons. Place cards in box.

Procedure

Divide group into pairs. Each pair picks a card form the box and plans a way to perform the puppet skit. (If there is an extra player, have him or her be the announcer for all the skits.) After several minutes each pair takes a turn performing a skit using the puppets. After each skit, ask class to tell how the puppets applied the truth of the lesson.

Two puppets are walking along and bump into each other.

One puppet has a bad cold and can't come out to play.

One puppet teases another puppet.

Actionary

Materials Checklist

- [ ] large decorated box or chest
- [ ] variety of items to use as props in skits (loaf of bread, purse, hat, pan, bandage, baseball bat, doll, Bible, stationery, etc.)

Preparation
None.

Procedure
Allow each student to choose an item from the box. Students then take turns performing short skits to illustrate the principle learned in that day's lesson. They may work in groups of two or three. The items chosen from the box must be used in the skit. (Skit theme ideas: Loving and helping others, God meets our needs, Forgiveness, God's help in temptation.) After each skit ask, **How did the skit remind you of what God is like?**

The Box of Many Uses

Materials Checklist

☐ one large, sturdy cardboard box

Preparation

None.

Procedure

Children take turns using the box to help reenact parts of the Bible story or create situations with modern-day applications to life. Encourage children to use their imaginations as they think of ways to use the box. Make suggestions only as needed. The scenes should be done impromptu. Ask, **What are some good things you can do with God's help?** Students use box to act out situations showing obedience, honesty, kindness, forgiveness, etc. (E.g., Act out raking leaves, picking up trash from yard and putting leaves and trash in "trash bin box.") Ask, **What are some ways people can show love to their enemies?** Students use box to act out situations contrasting kindness with "getting even." (E.g., Enemy—mean kid at school—has flat tire on bike. You and your mom drive by in "car box." You stop to offer ride.) Ask, **When are some good times for telling others about God?** Students use box to act out situations when they might tell others about God. (E.g., Friend is sick and lying on "bed box." Offer to pray for friend. Tell about God's power and love.)

Enrichment Idea: Have students try to guess the scene or situation being pantomimed. The student who guesses gets to act out the next scene.

Problem Solving

Materials Checklist
☐ pencils
☐ two sheets of paper

Preparation
None.

Procedure
Divide group into two teams and send each team to a different room (or as far apart as possible in the same room). Team one makes a list of 10 problems such as "My little brother always wants to play in my room." Team two makes a list of 20 solutions to problems such as "Tell the truth even when it's hard."

When children return to the room, a member of team one reads a problem and team two chooses the most appropriate solution and a team member reads it. Be prepared for some of the combinations not to fit exactly; and some may be humorous!

Review the Bible lesson. Say, **God can help you no matter what the situation. What are some ways He can help you?**

Variations: Team one writes funny problems such as "My feet grew three sizes overnight." Team two writes silly solutions such as "Brush them until they're white again." Children match problems with solutions in the funniest way. Then talk about how God can help each person with *real* problems.

Try a "backwards" variation. When teams return to the room, have children read a solution first, then the problem.

My little brother always wants to play in my room.

I didn't study for a test.

Tell the truth even when it's hard.

Share with the other person.

Junior Games

Rebus Review

Materials Checklist

- [ ] Bible
- [ ] pen
- [ ] one strip of paper for each child
- [ ] chalkboard and chalk or large sheet of butcher paper

Preparation

Choose a Bible story students have studied. On strips of paper list statements about events in the Bible story—one statement for each student.

Procedure

Give each player a paper strip. Students silently read statements and think of a symbol or drawing that represents the Bible story event. Teacher calls on individual students to draw their symbol on the chalkboard or paper. Students take turns guessing what each person's symbol means. Players can draw more than one symbol if necessary. However, the goal is to communicate the event in as few symbols as possible.

After each event is guessed, ask questions such as, **Who showed (respect) in this situation? What choices did this person have to make? Do you agree with his or her choices? Why or why not? In what situations do you choose to show (respect)?**

Junior/Bible Story Review

Three-Legged Chicken Game

Materials Checklist

- [ ] Bible
- [ ] two chairs
- [ ] paper
- [ ] pen
- [ ] two large index cards
- [ ] strips of cloth (one for every two children)
- [ ] tape

Preparation

Choose a Bible story students have studied. On a sheet of paper, list true or false statements about events in the Bible story. List one statement for every two children in your group. Letter one index card "True" and another "False." Tape labeled index cards to chairs placed between teams (sketch a).

Procedure

Divide class into two equal teams. (If you have an extra student, he or she may read aloud the true or false statements.) Each team divides into pairs. Pairs use clean cloth strips to tie inside legs together above the knee (sketch b). Pairs are assigned the name of a farm animal. Teams sit on floor as shown in sketch.

After teams are seated, leader reads aloud a statement about the Bible story and then calls out the name of a farm animal. The pairs with that animal's name jump up and run to sit in the "true" or "false" chair. The pair of players who sit in the correct chair first score a point for their team. In case of a tie, each team scores a point. Repeat process until all statements have been read. Pause to allow students to correct each false statement. When game is over, ask, **What does this story teach us about (joy)? What part of the story did you find most interesting? Why?**

a.

(TEAM A)
Chicken   Cow   Pig
False   True
Chicken   Cow   Pig
(TEAM B)

b.

Quick Draw

Materials Checklist

- [ ] Bible
- [ ] at least 10 small slips of paper
- [ ] pen
- [ ] box
- [ ] chair
- [ ] chalkboard and chalk or two large pads of paper and two felt pens

Preparation

On slips of paper write 10 or more words or phrases from a Bible story students have studied. (Example: Jesus, lawyer, rocks and hills, money, robbers, bruises and cuts, priest, donkey's hooves, Samaritan, inn.)

Procedure

Divide class into two teams and have each team sit on the floor as far away from each other as possible. Teams each choose one artist and one runner. Place chair between teams (see sketch). Leader stands in front near chalkboard or paper. At your signal, artist from each team runs up to the front and reads a slip of paper that leader is holding. Players quickly draw a picture of the word or phrase, without speaking or drawing letters or words. Teams try to guess the correct word or phrase. When a team has the correct answer, team runner quickly runs and sits in the chair and calls out word or phrase. Team gets one point and play starts over again. Teams choose a different artist and runner each time. When all words have been drawn, team with the most points wins. At end of game ask questions such as, **What did you learn about God from this story? Which character showed (kindness)? How?**

Junior/Bible Story Review
Guess What I'm Thinking...

Materials Checklist
None.

Preparation
None.

Procedure
Students sit in a circle as they play this game similar to "Twenty Questions." Choose a volunteer to begin. He or she thinks of a person, place or thing mentioned in the Bible story. Students attempt to guess the person, place or thing by asking questions of the volunteer that can be answered with "yes" or "no." Student who guesses correctly leads the next round. Student leader should write down the name to be guessed, giving it to a teacher who can assist as needed in responding correctly to questions.

We Got It!

Materials Checklist

- ☐ Bible
- ☐ large index cards
- ☐ felt pen

Preparation

Letter the alphabet on index cards—one letter on each card. Omit the letters *Q* and *X*. Make two sets of alphabet cards.

Procedure

Divide the group into two teams. Give each team a set of alphabet cards to be divided as evenly as possible among team members. You will then call out a word or name from the session's Bible story. The players with those letters must arrange themselves to correctly spell the word. (A player who is holding two or more letters used in the word must reach around other players to hold those letters in the correct order. A player who is holding a letter which is used more than once must stand at the first position where the letter occurs.) As soon as the team members think they are in the correct order, they yell, "We got it!" The other team must then freeze in position. The players on the first team who are not holding letters used in their word then spell the word aloud. If a player is holding a letter used more than once, he or she must run back into the next position(s) where the letter appears as the word is spelled aloud. Correct spelling is worth ten points, but an error deducts five—and the other team gets to attempt the correct spelling. When word has been spelled correctly, have a player tell its meaning or explain how the word was used in the Bible story. (*Hint:* Play a practice round before you begin keeping score.)

Geo-Tales

Materials Checklist

- ☐ Bible
- ☐ large sheets of drawing paper and felt pen or chalkboard and chalk
- ☐ letter-sized paper
- ☐ pencils

Preparation

None.

Procedure

Divide class into teams of four to six students. Secretly, assign each team an event or scene from the Bible story. Using letter-sized paper, teams practice sketching their events/scenes using only geometric shapes (circles, rectangles, triangles, half circles). They must use at least 10 separate shapes (see sketch).

Play begins as members of first team begin to draw scene on large paper or chalkboard. Other teams try to guess the scene. If the scene is guessed after one shape is drawn, the guessing team as well as the drawing team get 100 points each. If scene is guessed after two shapes, each team gets 90 points. After 3 shapes, teams get 80 and so on. If after ten shapes are drawn no team has guessed correctly, no points are scored and it is the next team's turn to draw. After all teams have drawn, team with the highest total score is the winner.

Clay Bible Scenes

Materials Checklist

- [ ] play dough
- [ ] table
- [ ] stopwatch
- [ ] slips of paper
- [ ] pencil

Preparation

On each of three different slips of paper, letter brief descriptions of scenes from the Bible story (see sketch for example). Number the cards according to their order of appearance in the story. Place three large lumps of play dough on a table.

Procedure

Divide group into three teams. Give each team a slip of paper describing a scene from the Bible story of the lesson you are teaching. Teams line up on the opposite end of the room from the table. When the teacher gives a signal the first member of each team runs to the table and begins to construct his or her team's Bible story scene from clay. Teacher sets stopwatch for 30 seconds. When time is up the next person in line has 30 seconds to add to the creation. When all members of each team have contributed, the scenes should be complete. (To accomplish this, you may need to adjust the time limit or give each student two turns, depending on the size of each group.) Then allow team members to tell the Bible story. Group holding card 1 can tell the beginning of the story, up to the scene on card 2. Group with card 2 tells story up to the scene on card 3. The last group concludes the story.

Older son is jealous when dad throws a party.

Youngest son works in a pig pen.

Youngest son asks father for money.

Junior/Bible Story Review

Who Said That?

Materials Checklist

- [ ] cassette recorder and blank cassette tape
- [ ] chalk and chalkboard

Preparation

Record various phrases that were spoken by characters in one or more Bible stories. You may want to use a different voice for each phrase.

Procedure

Divide group into two teams. Play first recorded phrase from Bible story. Then ask, **"Who said it?"** The first person to stand may answer to gain 100 points for his or her team. Next ask, **"Why did he (or she) say it?"** Again, the first person to stand may answer the question to gain points for his or her team. Then ask, **"What happened next?"** Record points on chalkboard. Continue until all phrases have been identified.

Balloon Bust

Materials Checklist

- ☐ cassette tape of children's songs
- ☐ cassette player
- ☐ beanbag or sponge ball
- ☐ balloons
- ☐ tape
- ☐ paper
- ☐ pencil
- ☐ a chair for each student

Preparation

Arrange chairs in a circle. On small slips of paper write various statements from the Bible story—one for each student. Leave out one key word in each statement. For example: "The prodigal son spent all his money on ____ living." "Philip explained the ____ to a man from Ethiopia." Place each slip of paper inside a balloon. Inflate balloons and attach to chairs with tape.

Procedure

Students sit in chairs. As cassette is played, students toss beanbag randomly around or across the circle. When the music stops, whoever has the beanbag pops the balloon taped to his or her chair and reads the sentence, filling in the blank. (If the student is unable to fill in the blank, student passes the beanbag to the person on his or her right.) Play continues until all the balloons have been popped. (If a student has already popped his or her balloon and is left holding the beanbag, it should be passed to another student.) Be sure to instruct your students to use caution when passing the beanbag.

Timer Tales

Materials Checklist

☐ kitchen timer or watch that indicates seconds

Preparation

None.

Procedure

Students sit on chairs in a circle. Teacher sets timer for 15 seconds and the first student begins telling the Bible story. When the timer rings, the first student must stop mid-sentence and the second student picks up where he or she left off. Reset the timer. Story-telling continues in this manner until the complete story is told.

Variation: Have students create a modern version of the Bible story using present-day people and situations. After the storytelling ask, **Why do you think God wanted this story to be in the Bible? What is one important thing you think you'll remember from this story? Why is it important?**

Invent-a-Language

Materials Checklist

- [ ] Bible
- [ ] chalkboard and chalk or butcher paper and felt pen
- [ ] paper and pencils

Preparation

Letter Bible memory verse on chalkboard or paper.

Procedure

Divide class into teams of two to three students. Pass out paper and pencils. Each team invents their own kind of language by developing a new rule to the English language. For example, take the last letter from a word and add it to the beginning, then add -ich to the end of the word. ("Verse" becomes "eversich.") Teacher sets a time limit and groups practice saying the Bible verse using their new language. Each group presents their verse to the class, while class tries to figure out the group's language rule. Say, **Learning new languages can be fun! Now that we know everyone's "new language," let's talk about the verse. What does this verse say to you?** Ask volunteers to explain the meanings of some of the more difficult words.

Street Musician Coin Toss

Materials Checklist

- [ ] Bible
- [ ] live musician or cassette tape of children's songs
- [ ] cassette player
- [ ] paper cups
- [ ] felt pen
- [ ] pennies
- [ ] empty musical instrument case
- [ ] measuring stick

Preparation

Letter words of verse on paper cups—two to three words on each cup. Place cups in a row, in mixed-up order, inside the instrument case with top of case open. Use masking tape to mark a line on the floor about 4 feet (1.2 m) from case.

Procedure

Ask, **Who has heard a street musician? What instrument was the person playing? Did the musician have a cup or instrument case open for people to toss in donations?** Distribute several pennies to each student. Explain that students will take turns tossing coins into instrument case as music plays. Students line up behind line. While musician or cassette plays, first player tries to toss a penny into first cup. He or she then goes to back of line and second player tosses pennies until one lands in second cup. Game continues until all players have had a chance to toss their pennies. When game is completed have students read aloud the verse in correct order. Ask, **What part of this verse seems most important to you? Why? What did you learn from this verse?**

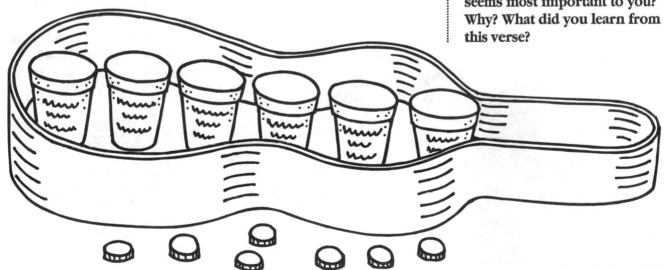

Wheelbarrow Relay

Materials Checklist

- [ ] Bible
- [ ] index cards
- [ ] felt pen
- [ ] paper
- [ ] two baskets
- [ ] masking tape

Preparation

Letter words of a Bible memory verse on index cards—two words on each card. Make an additional set of cards. with masking tape, mark on the floor a start and a finish line 30 feet (9 m) apart. Place baskets on finish line.

Procedure

Place one set of index cards in order on the floor and read verse aloud with children. Repeat several times. Collect cards. Divide group into two teams. Teams line up on starting line. Place a stack of verse cards (in order) by the first player on each team. At starting signal, first child on each team places the top index card between his or her teeth. Child then assumes "wheelbarrow position" and walks on hands toward the basket, while next child in line steers the "wheelbarrow" by holding his or her feet (see sketch). Child drops card into basket. Children then switch positions and return to the back of starting line. Before next pair may go, first pair says the words that were on their card. When second pair returns to line, they say the first two words, and the second two words. Continue process with third pair. Play continues until entire memory verse is recited. (Pairs may need to take several turns.)

Ask, **How can remembering this verse help you? How would you say this verse in your own words?**

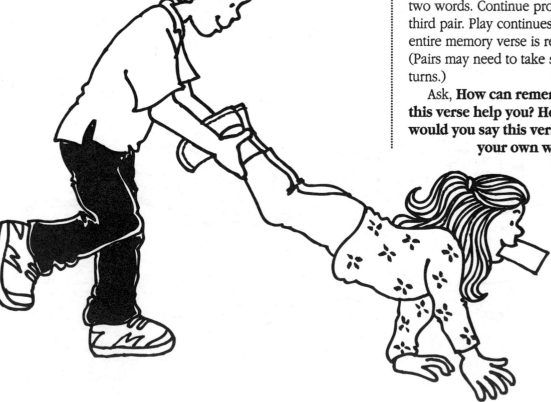

Junior/Bible Memory Verse Review

Tattoo You

Materials Checklist

- [ ] small blank stickers
- [ ] felt pen
- [ ] pencil and paper for keeping score

Preparation

Write each of the following letters on a separate sticker—*l, o, v, e, j, o, y, p, a, c, e, t, i, n, k, d, n, s, s.* Make two sets of stickers. (*Optional:* Include additional letters to spell the words "goodness," "faithfulness," "gentleness" and "self-control.")

Procedure

Divide class into two teams and have teams sit in lines on the floor. Place one set of stickers on the foreheads of players on Team A. Do the same for players on Team B. (You will probably need to place two or three stickers on each player. Don't give one player two vowels or two of the same letter.) To play the game, call out one fruit of the Spirit (love, joy, peace, patience, kindness).

Appropriate players on each team stand up and arrange themselves in order to spell the word. (If a player has two of the necessary letters, he or she may quickly give one to another team member.) The first team to complete the word scores a point. Bonus points may be scored by either or both teams if one of the players can name a way a person might demonstrate that characteristic at church (home, school, etc.). To help students, ask questions such as, **How might a person show that he or she has peace? When could a person be patient? Kind?**

Verse Olympics

Materials Checklist

- [ ] Bible
- [ ] five hole punchers
- [ ] index cards
- [ ] paper
- [ ] felt pens
- [ ] stapler and staples
- [ ] scissors
- [ ] masking tape
- [ ] photocopier

For each of five stations one of the following:

- [ ] mini-trampoline
- [ ] Ping-Pong paddle and Ping-Pong ball
- [ ] jump rope
- [ ] stationary exercise bike
- [ ] exercise mat
- [ ] balloon
- [ ] rubber ball
- [ ] unicycle

Preparation

Letter the references for Bible verses recently memorized on each index card—one for each student. Prepare five signs for five stations. (See sketch for station suggestions.) Attach signs to walls at different stations throughout the room. Place appropriate props at each station. Arrange to have a student or teacher at each station to listen to verses and punch holes in verse cards.

Procedure

Give each student a verse card. Students visit each station and follow instructions on signs. The station helpers punch holes in students' verse cards when they have completed assigned tasks.

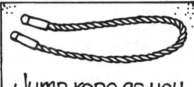

Jump rope as you recite Proverbs 2:6.

Do sit ups as you recite Proverbs 13:20.

Touch your toes as you recite Proverbs 14:15.

Stand on one foot as you recite Proverbs 12:15.

With a partner, find Proverbs 3:5,6 in the Bible. Read it aloud together.

Bounce Back Verse

Materials Checklist

- [ ] Bible
- [ ] Ping-Pong table, 2 paddles, Ping-Pong ball; or chalk, rubber ball and an asphalt play area

Preparation

Set up Ping-Pong table or draw a two-square game on the asphalt.

Procedure

Divide group into two teams. Teams line up on opposite sides of Ping-Pong table or two-square court. First player says first word of the Bible Memory Verse as he or she hits the Ping-Pong ball across table. First player on second team says second word of verse while hitting ball back. After hitting the ball, players go to the end of the line. Play until verse has been repeated several times, or as interest allows. (If a student misses the ball, allow him or her to try again with the same word. Students who miss should not be forced to go back to beginning of verse.)

(*Optional:* Have students form a circle around table and continually rotate clockwise after each hit. A player who misses a word—or the ball—is out for the rest of the round. The game can get heated when down to just a few players.)

Verse Commercials

Materials Checklist
- [ ] Bibles
- [ ] paper
- [ ] pencils

Optional—
- [ ] video camera
- [ ] blank video tape
- [ ] VCR and TV

Preparation
None.

Procedure
Students form groups of three to five members. Assign each group a Bible memory verse to read in their Bibles. All groups may read the same verse or you may choose to have each group review a different verse from the unit. Groups read assigned verses and create 20- or 60-second Verse Commercials that attempt to convince the audience of the truth found in their verse. Each commercial should show how the truth of the verse will affect the lives of those who believe it or obey it. To help groups get started, ask questions such as, **What is the main idea of this verse? What are some slogans or jingles that would encourage someone to obey this verse? When is a time you need to remember this verse?** (You may want to have several teachers perform a commercial or two to help inspire your students.) Group members work together as they write down ideas for their commercial and rehearse it. Then groups perform commercials for each other. *Optional:* Videotape commercials and watch them as a review of the Bible memory verses and their applications.

Junior/Bible Memory Verse Review

Musical Verse

Materials Checklist

- ☐ cassette tape of children's songs
- ☐ cassette player
- ☐ large index cards
- ☐ felt pens
- ☐ masking tape

Preparation

Letter a Bible memory verse on cards—one word or short phrase on each card.

Procedure

Give each student a set of six index cards and a felt pen. Instruct students to letter the Bible memory verse on cards as you have done in your example. Students use tape to attach cards randomly on the walls of the room (see sketch).

Students form a large circle, standing next to the four walls of the room. As music is played, students walk clockwise around the room. When music stops, students have three seconds to run and touch any verse card and freeze. (Teacher may count to three, then call "freeze.") When music begins again, students may "unfreeze," remove cards they have touched (beginning personal collections of verse cards) and begin walking around the room again. Any student caught moving after the teacher calls "freeze" must put one of his or her cards back up on the wall. Play continues until one student collects all the cards he or she needs to complete verse.

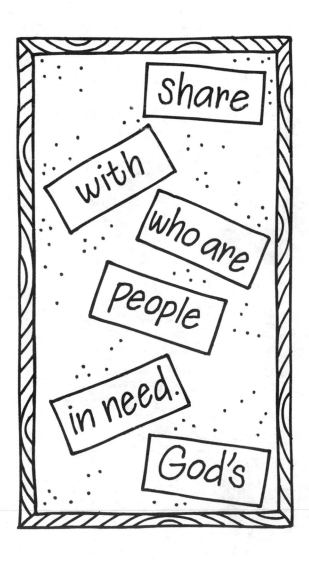

Share with who are people in need. God's

Memory Verse Chant

Materials Checklist
None.

Preparation
None.

Procedure

Review the Bible memory verse by saying it rhythmically. Lead group in using hands to create the rhythm by slapping legs once, clapping hands once, snapping fingers of right hand then left hand. When students are comfortable with the rhythm, add words of the Bible Memory Verse. Say one word of verse on each beat. Challenge students by having them speed up rhythm or go around circle, each person adding a word to the verse on the beat.

Variations: Group divides to form teams. Each group creates its own unique rhythm sequence (e.g., two hand claps, one leg slap, snap both fingers). Teams then practice rhythm with Bible verse to present to the class.

Or have teams create hand motions ("finger fun") to go with the verse. Each day another verse is added until all five verses have been combined to form one long finger play.

Tic-Tac-Toe Verse Review

Materials Checklist

- [ ] Bible
- [ ] masking tape
- [ ] construction paper
- [ ] felt pen

Preparation

Use masking tape to create a tic-tac-toe grid on the floor. Make squares large enough for students to stand in. On each piece of construction paper, letter one of the following statements or questions:

Say the verse from memory.

Look up the verse.

What does the verse mean?

Where is the verse found in the Bible?

Give an example of a way to do what the verse says.

Say the first half of the verse.

Say the last half of the verse.

Who said the verse?

Who is the verse talking to?

Tape one of the questions inside each square of the tic-tac-toe grid.

Procedure

Divide group into two teams. The first team sends a member to stand in one square. That student follows the instructions in his or her square as it relates to the Bible memory verse. If correct, team member stands in square until round is over. Teams take turns until one team has formed a tic-tac-toe (three squares in a row).

Variation: Draw a tic-tac-toe grid on a sheet of paper. Letter the statements above randomly in squares. Make a photocopy for each player. Students use pencils or makers to mark *X*s and *O*s on papers.

Writin' Relay

Materials Checklist

- [ ] masking tape
- [ ] chalkboard and chalk or newsprint, felt pens and tape

Preparation

Letter the reference for the Bible memory verse on chalkboard. Use masking tape to mark a line on the floor at least 15 feet (4.5 m) from chalkboard.

Procedure

Review the Bible Memory Verse with students. This will help them succeed in the game. Ask, **Why is it good to know Bible verses from memory? When might this verse help you?** Divide class into two or more teams. Each team lines up behind designated line. Give a piece of chalk to the first player on each team. When teacher says "go," the first member of each team runs to the chalkboard and writes the first word of the Bible memory verse. He or she then runs back to the line and passes the chalk to the next member of the team who writes the second word. If a mistake has been made, a player may use his or her turn to correct the mistake. Play continues until one team has written the complete verse correctly and all members are seated on the floor signifying that they are finished. *Variation:* Have players hop on one foot to the chalkboard or walk backwards.

For God so loved   For God so"

Back and Forth

Materials Checklist
☐ balloons

Preparation
Inflate several balloons.

Procedure
Review the Bible memory verse. Divide class into two teams. Teams line up on designated line. A teacher stands across the room from each team and holds a balloon. At a given signal, the first two players on each team run over to their teacher and take the balloon. They then recite the Bible memory verse as they hit the balloon back and forth, each player saying a word as he or she hits the balloon. The teacher listens to make sure the verse is said correctly. The pair then runs back to the team and another pair repeats the process. The play continues until all team members have participated. The team who finishes first wins. When game is over and students are resting ask, **Why is this an important verse to know? How can this verse make a difference in a person's life?** *Variation:* You may want to have players say verse in trios to take pressure off slower students.

Off-the-Wall Ball

Materials Checklist

- [ ] Bible
- [ ] high-bounce rubber ball (such as a hand ball)
- [ ] chalk
- [ ] drinking straws
- [ ] scissors
- [ ] measuring stick

Preparation

This game requires the use of an unobstructed wall. On a paved area, use chalk to draw an 8-foot (2.4-m) square handball court extending from the base of the wall as shown in sketch. Letter the words of Bible memory verse on the wall as shown. Cut drinking straws into various lengths—one for each student.

Procedure

Read verse aloud with students. Repeat several times.

Players draw straws. The player who draws the longest straw is the server or "king" and serves first. Other players line up, according to the length of their straws, near the right edge of court. The king starts the game by reciting the first word of verse, entering into the handball court and bouncing the ball once on the ground so it hits the wall. The king runs to the end of the line as the next player in line enters the court, allowing the ball to bounce on the ground once, and recites the second word of verse before hitting the ball back to the wall for the next player. The ball must bounce only once before hitting the wall and only once before the next player can hit it. If player allows the ball to bounce on the ground more than once or hits the ball out of court or cannot recite the next word in the verse before hitting the ball, he or she proceeds to the end of the lineup. The king then starts the game and the verse over again with other players keeping their current positions in line. The object of the game is to recite the entire verse.

" Honor your father and your mother as the Lord your God has commanded you." Deut. 5:16

8'

8'

Junior/Bible Memory Verse Review

Jam-on-It

Materials Checklist

- ☐ Bible
- ☐ two tricycles
- ☐ chalk and chalkboard
- ☐ two chalkboard erasers
- ☐ colored chalk or masking tape
- ☐ measuring stick

Preparation

Letter words of Bible memory verse twice on chalkboard, once on the right side and once on the left. Place erasers on chalkboard tray.

Use chalk or tape to mark a starting line 20 feet (6 m) from the chalkboard. Mark two roads on the floor from starting line to the chalkboard (see sketch).

Procedure

Read verse aloud with students. Repeat several times.

Divide class into two even teams. Teams line up behind starting line. First player on each team pedals tricycle along the road to the chalkboard. Player then erases one word of the memory verse and pedals tricycle back to the starting line following the same road as team recites entire verse aloud. Second player on each team then takes his or her turn to erase a word. Game continues until all words have been erased and team recites entire verse.

Hopscotch Relay

Materials Checklist

☐ Bible

☐ two pieces of chalk

☐ two margarine tub lids

☐ felt pen

Preparation

Letter the words of Bible memory verse on each lid. On outdoor paved area, use chalk to draw two identical hopscotch diagrams as shown in sketch. Place lid and chalk in last square.

Procedure

Read verse together. Divide class into two teams. Teams line up at hopscotch diagrams. First player from each team hops through hopscotch, hopping on one foot in single blocks and two feet in double blocks. Upon reaching last square, player leans over on one foot and picks up chalk and lid. He or she then proceeds to write the first word of memory verse in end circle. Player then returns chalk and lid to last square and hops back through hopscotch to tag the next player who repeats process, writing next word of verse in circle. The first team to complete entire memory verse and return to line wins. Repeat game as time allows.

Skippin' Street Smarts

Materials Checklist

- [ ] Bible
- [ ] chalkboard and chalk or poster board and felt pen
- [ ] a long jump rope

Preparation

Letter Bible memory verse on chalkboard or poster board as shown in sketch.

Procedure

Using rhythm as shown in example (each number equals one beat), read verse aloud with students. Repeat several times.

Choose two assistants or students to twirl the jump rope. Jumpers line up behind a designated starting point. First player tries to jump in and over the rope as the rope is twirled slowly. Once the first jumper is in and jumping steadily, the next player enters. Players continue to enter the game until space is filled (usually about six to seven jumpers). Then all students recite memory verse in rhythm as players jump. Play continues until all students have had a turn or until time is up.

Variation: For easier jump roping, players may jump individually or players may simply swing rope back and forth.

Every-one should be quick to listen, slow to speak, and slow to become an-gry.
James 1:19

Crazy Eights

Materials Checklist

- [ ] Bible
- [ ] eight metal bottle caps
- [ ] chalk
- [ ] measuring stick

Preparation

On a paved area, use chalk to draw eight large squares in various locations, at least 8 feet (2.4 m) apart. Letter the words of Bible memory verse in squares—one phrase in each square (see sketch). Number the squares 1–8. Draw a starting line and a small circle about 10 feet (3 m) from square one.

Procedure

Read verse aloud with students. Repeat several times.

Players line up on starting line and recite verse in unison. Teacher gently throws all the bottle caps into the air, above the circle. Players quickly count how many bottle caps land inside the circle and race to the square with that same number. The first player to reach the square gets to stay there, while the other players return to the starting line. Players recite verse again, pausing to allow player in the square to say his or her phrase alone. Repeat process until entire verse is recited phrase by phrase. (*Note:* When tossing bottle caps results in a repeated number, another player may be added to that square. Teacher tries to flip bottle caps so that all squares become filled.)

The Grape Touchdown

Materials Checklist

- [ ] Bible
- [ ] chalkboard and chalk or large sheet of paper and a felt pen
- [ ] masking tape or tacks
- [ ] three or four purple balloons
- [ ] cluster of grapes with part of vine or long stem attached

Preparation

Letter the words of Bible memory verse on chalkboard or sheet of paper. Display verse chart in visible location. Inflate balloons and tie.

Procedure

Recite the verse aloud with students several times, referring to chalkboard or chart. Divide class into groups of five or six students. (Some children may be more comfortable in same-sex groups.) Groups spread out around room and stand in circles, holding on to each others' wrists. Give each group a balloon and say, **Imagine each group is a vine, and the balloon is the grape. The object of the game is to stay connected. Don't let go of each other or let the grape touch the ground.** Have groups practice tapping balloon into the air while holding each others' wrists, then begin game. One student taps the balloon into the air while saying the first word of the memory verse. The person who is closest to where the balloon is falling taps it up again and says the second word in the verse, and so on. Students may use any part of their body to keep the balloon in the air, but must continue to hold wrists. If the balloon lands between two people, and both hit the balloon up, then both students say the word together. Once verse is completed, students may start over again. If the balloon hits the ground, or players let go of wrists, group begins verse over. Groups keep count of how many times the verse is completed. Share the results.

(*Optional:* Cover up or erase two or three words of the verse each time you play to make it more difficult.)

In Search of Joy

Materials Checklist

- [ ] Bible
- [ ] four sheets of construction paper—red, blue, yellow and green
- [ ] four pieces of tissue paper or cellophane—red, blue, yellow and green
- [ ] four rubber bands
- [ ] scissors
- [ ] felt pen
- [ ] four flashlights
- [ ] several different sizes of cardboard boxes
- [ ] chalkboard and chalk or large sheet of paper

Preparation

Place each piece of tissue paper over a flashlight lens and secure with rubber band (see sketch). Cut yellow sheet of construction paper into eight equal pieces. Letter Bible memory verse on construction paper—two words on each piece. Use other colors of construction paper to make three additional verse sets. Place boxes in various locations around the room. Hide verse papers in fairly easy-to-find locations such as in boxes, under chairs or tables, in corners and on shelves. Letter verse on chalkboard or paper. Cover windows and turn off lights to darken room. (If classroom cannot be darkened, play game in a darker room, such as fellowship hall or basement classroom.)

Procedure

Recite memory verse aloud with students. Divide class into four teams—red, yellow, green and blue team. Give each team a corresponding flashlight. The four teams search for the pieces of the verse, using their flashlights. Teams keep only their own color of papers. Encourage team members to take turns holding flashlights. When teams have found complete set of verse pieces, members work together to put words in order. The game is over when teacher turns lights on.

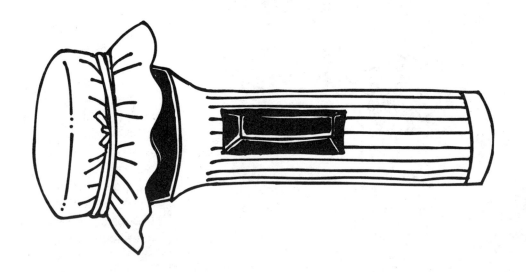

Sign It to Me

Materials Checklist
- [ ] Bible
- [ ] chalkboard and chalk or butcher paper and felt pen

Preparation
Letter Bible memory verse on chalkboard or paper.

Procedure
Read verse aloud with students. Divide class into groups of four or five students. Groups gather in different parts of the room and create "sign language" movements for each word of the verse. When finished, each group presents its version to the class. Encourage students to think of unique ways to present their signs (simultaneously, one person at a time, in a single-file line, etc.).

" Serve the Lord with all your heart. "
1 Sam. 12:20

Farm Feud

Materials Checklist

- [ ] Bible
- [ ] chalkboard and chalk or butcher paper and felt pens
- [ ] two game bells
- [ ] paper and pencil
- [ ] small table
- [ ] chair for each student
- [ ] two farmer hats

Preparation

Letter the words of Bible memory verse on the chalkboard or butcher paper. Place chairs in two rows facing each other. Place table at head of lines. Place game bells on table. (See sketch.)

On a piece of paper write several situations in which someone might actively demonstrate kindness (or other word that relates to your verse), such as: Your friend just won the spelling bee. You...; Your little sister fell and scraped her knee. You...; Everybody is making fun of the kid sitting in front of you because someone taped a sign on his back. You...; etc. Write at least one situation for every two students.

Procedure

Read verse aloud with students. Repeat several times. This game is similar to Family Feud. Divide class into two teams. Teams sit in chairs facing each other. First member of each team wears a farm hat and stands by bell, with hands behind back (see sketch). Teacher reads a situation aloud. First player to hit the bell finishes the sentence, describing a way to show kindness in that situation. Player who answers wins that round and his or her team is given the opportunity to recite memory verse. Team recites memory verse starting with first player saying first word, passing hat to second player who puts it on his or her head while saying second word, and so on. A point is given if team says memory verse without any mistakes. Game continues as second players from each team play next round.

Junior/Bible Memory Verse Review

Scrolls in a Jar

Materials Checklist

- [ ] Bible
- [ ] brown wrapping paper or paper grocery bags
- [ ] scissors
- [ ] string or yarn
- [ ] felt pen
- [ ] two large clay pots
- [ ] two beanbags
- [ ] two rolls of tape

Preparation

Letter the words of Bible memory verse on large rectangle cut from paper bag and display in a visible location. Repeat to make two more verse charts. Cut these into 16 pieces each—one word on each piece. Roll paper pieces into scrolls and tie with string or yarn. Place one set of 16 scrolls in each pot. Place pots on floor. (Option for small groups: Make only two verse charts. Display one chart and cut apart the second chart. Put first eight pieces in one jar, last eight in other jar.)

Procedure

Read verse aloud with students. Divide group into two teams. Give each team a roll of tape. Teams line up six to eight feet from pots. First student on each team tosses beanbag into clay pot. (Student gets as many tries as necessary to get beanbag in pot.) When beanbag lands in pot, student runs to the pot, removes a scroll and the beanbag and runs back to his or her team. The beanbag is given to the next person in line who repeats process. When all scrolls are removed from the pot, each team works together to tape words in order and recite verse together.

Creatures Speak

Materials Checklist

- [ ] Bibles
- [ ] large sheets of butcher paper or poster board
- [ ] felt pens
- [ ] scissors
- [ ] large paper bags
- [ ] tape or tacks

Preparation

Letter Bible memory verse on butcher paper or poster board and display in visible location.

Procedure

Read verse aloud with students. Divide group into pairs. Working together, each pair outlines a large animal on sheet of paper or poster board and letters the words to verse inside the animal outline (see sketch). Students then cut animal into about twelve puzzle pieces and place pieces in bag. Each pair exchanges bags with another pair. Pairs remove puzzles from bags and work together to complete puzzles and memorize verse. **What two important truths do we learn from this verse?** (Students respond.)

"Know that the Lord is God. It is he who made us, and we are his." Psalm 100:3

Bible Words Bounce

Materials Checklist

- ☐ Bible
- ☐ chalkboard and chalk or butcher paper
- ☐ felt pen and tape or tacks
- ☐ two basketballs or rubber balls
- ☐ large play area

Preparation

Letter words of Bible memory verse on chalkboard or butcher paper and display in a visible location.

Procedure

Read verse aloud with students. Repeat verse several times. Divide class into two teams. Each team forms two lines which stand about 8 feet (2.4 m) apart facing each other (see sketch). Teams practice bounce-passing ball back and forth between lines (see sketch). At a signal, teams compete to pass ball, saying a word of the verse with each pass. Remove verse poster, then play game several more times.

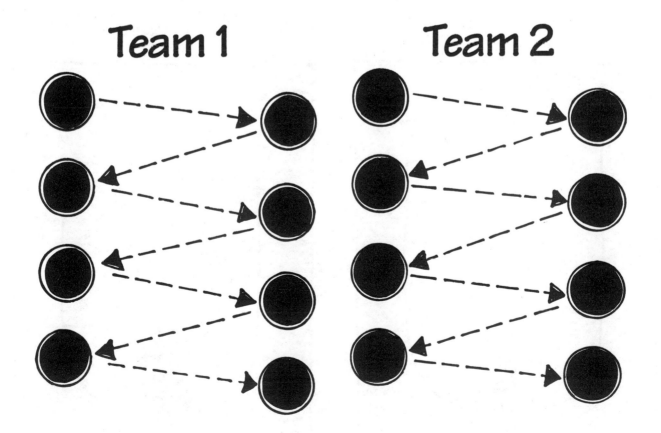

Pulled from the Pit

Materials Checklist

- [ ] Bible
- [ ] three large sheets of poster board
- [ ] felt pen
- [ ] construction paper
- [ ] scissors
- [ ] masking tape

Preparation

Letter words of Bible memory verse on one sheet of poster board. On each remaining sheet of poster board, draw an outline of a pit. Draw lines up one side of each pit, one line for each team member. From construction paper, cut two simple outlines of a person. Attach a loop of tape to the back of each figure and secure to the bottom of each pit. Attach sheets of poster board to wall.

Procedure

Read verse aloud with students. A teacher or helper stands next to each "pit." Divide group into two equal teams. Each team lines up opposite a "pit." At a signal, the first two players on each team run to their pit. They recite the verse to the teacher or helper, each player saying alternate words. If students successfully recite verse, the teacher moves the figure up to the next line on the pit. Players run back to their team and tag the next two players in line, who repeat process. Continue until all players have had a turn and the man has been rescued from the pit.

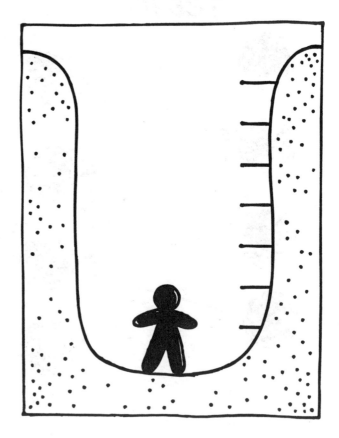

Words in Stone

Materials Checklist

- [ ] Bible
- [ ] stones
- [ ] permanent felt pen

Preparation

Letter the words of Bible memory verse on stones—one word on each stone. Set stones in correct order on floor or table.

Procedure

Students read verse aloud several times. Then divide class into two teams. First team hides stones outside or in classroom. Time second team as they find stones and put the verse in order. Repeat with second team hiding the stones.

Rhythmic Verse

Materials Checklist

- [ ] Bible
- [ ] sheet of poster board
- [ ] felt pen
- [ ] variety of rhythm instruments
- [ ] tape or tacks

Preparation

Letter words to Bible memory verse on poster board and display in visible location.

Procedure

Read verse aloud with students. Divide class into groups of three to five students. Pass out rhythm instruments. Groups move to separate areas of room or building, then group members work together to practice saying verse rhythmically. Students use rhythm instruments to emphasize certain words or create a pattern of sounds to accompany words. Groups perform rhythmic versions of verse for the rest of class.

Illustrate the Verse

Materials Checklist

- ☐ Bibles
- ☐ long sheet of butcher paper
- ☐ felt pens
- ☐ tape or tacks

Preparation

To make mural, letter words to Bible memory verse across top of butcher paper (see sketch). Attach mural to wall or place on floor or table. For a large class, make two murals.

Procedure

Read verse aloud with students. Divide class into five (or ten) groups. Each group illustrates a portion of verse on mural. When groups are finished, volunteers may tell about their drawings. Repeat verse several times.

For to us a child is born, to us a son is given...	And he will be called Wonderful Counselor,	Mighty God,

Verse in Time

Materials Checklist

- [ ] Bible
- [ ] felt pen
- [ ] sheet of butcher paper
- [ ] tape or tacks

Preparation

Letter words of Bible memory verse on butcher paper. Attach paper to wall.

Procedure

Students sit in a circle. Lead students in creating a continuous rhythm by slapping thighs twice, clapping hands once and snapping fingers once (slap, slap, clap, snap). Each time you "snap," say a word of the verse in unison. When students are familiar with the verse and rhythm, they take turns around the circle saying a word of the verse as group continues rhythm.

Optional: If group does well at keeping the verse going with the rhythm, allow them to make up their own rhythmic pattern or increase the pace.

Junior/Bible Memory Verse Review

Sand Writing

Materials Checklist

- [ ] Bible
- [ ] index cards
- [ ] felt pen
- [ ] wet sand
- [ ] two large baking pans or cookie sheets
- [ ] two pencils
- [ ] newspapers

Preparation

Letter words to Bible memory verse on index cards—one word on each card. Make two sets. Stack each set of cards in order. Fill each baking pan or cookie sheet with wet sand. Place on tables or floor or on ground if playing outside. Place newspapers under pans. Place stacks of index cards face up across room from pans (see sketch).

Procedure

Repeat verse several times with students. Divide class into two teams. Each team lines up next to a pan of sand. At a signal, one member of each team runs to stack, takes the top card, runs back to pan and uses pencil to write first word of verse in sand. Team members say word aloud, then player "erases" word. Team members take turns running to get cards and writing words of verse in sand. First team to complete process and say the entire verse is the winner.

pan of sand

stack of cards

Disappearing Words

Materials Checklist

- [ ] Bible
- [ ] sheets of construction paper
- [ ] felt pens
- [ ] two number cubes
- [ ] one small treat for each student

Preparation

Letter sheets of construction paper with verse as shown in example in sketch. Lay verse in order on floor or table.

Procedure

Students gather around verse and read it aloud several times. Divide class into two teams. A volunteer from one team rolls one or both number cubes, turns over construction paper sheet with corresponding number and chooses a member of opposite team to read the verse, filling in the missing portion from memory. If player recites verse correctly, his or her team receives 10 points. This player then rolls the number cube(s) and turns over another phrase of the verse. If the number rolled has already been turned over, student may choose any other phrase. Play continues until all phrases have been turned over and students can recite verse from memory. Give a treat to each player whose team scored 50 points or more.

1 "And if	**2** I go	**3** and prepare
4 a place for you,	**5** I will	**6** come back
7 and take you	**8** to be with me	**9** that you also
10 may be	**11** where I am."	**12** John 14:3

Sign Here, Please

Materials Checklist

- ☐ Bible
- ☐ chalkboard and chalk or large sheet of paper and felt marker

Preparation

On the chalkboard or a large sheet of paper, letter the Bible memory verse in three lines. For example:

Everyone who believes in Him
Receives forgiveness of sins
Through His name.

Procedure

Lead the group in saying the verse in unison, establishing an easy, poetic rhythm. After several repetitions, ask the group to suggest possible gestures to use in place of any of the words in the verse. (For example, "everyone" could be shown with outstretched arms, "who believes" could be both hands brought together, palms up, etc.) Practice saying the verse together using the gestures. Then repeat the verse, except for the last word, which you replace with its gesture. Continue repeating the verse, each time dropping off one more word, replacing it with a gesture. Finally, you should be able to "say" the verse silently with motions.

Convertible Bible Verse

Materials Checklist

- ☐ Bible
- ☐ long strips of heavy paper cut to three inches in width
- ☐ felt pen
- ☐ scissors

Preparation

Letter Bible memory verse on strip(s) of paper so that letters touch the top and bottom edges of the strip. Then cut strips horizontally so that letters are cut in half. Vertically cut the top and bottom strips into pieces so that there are several pieces for each student. Make the vertical cuts in different places so the edges vary between the top and bottom pieces (see sketch). Stack all the pieces facedown in the center of the group.

Procedure

Explain that the pieces all have either the tops or bottoms of letters which appear in today's Bible memory verse. Select a player who begins by drawing the top piece from the stack and placing it faceup on the table or floor. The next player draws a piece and tries to connect it to the original piece. If the piece does not connect, it is placed faceup nearby. If the piece does connect, the player who correctly places it scores 10 points. As players take turns, more and more pieces are placed faceup, increasing the options for connecting. If a piece is placed incorrectly, the next player may place it in the correct position to gain 10 points.

When students have put the verse together, read verse aloud.

ACCEPT ONE ANOTHER, THEN, JUST AS CHRIST ← cut

ACCEPTED YOU, IN ORDER TO BRING PRAISE TO GOD. ← cut

Verse in Motion

Materials Checklist

- ☐ Bible
- ☐ large sheet of paper and masking tape or chalkboard and chalk
- ☐ sheets of drawing paper and felt pens

Preparation

Letter Bible memory verse on large piece of paper or chalkboard. Draw a symbol for one of the letters, such as the *o* in "world" as a large world globe.

Procedure

Give a sheet of paper and felt pen to each student or pair of students. Assign each student (or pair) one or two of the words in the Bible memory verse. Call attention to your drawing. Say, **This globe in the middle of "world" is a good way to help remember the word. Your job is to think of a way to write your word so one or more of the letters become a picture which illustrate that word.** Students complete assignment. Be ready with a few suggestions to stimulate students' ideas. (For example: **Go**—make the *o* the green light in a traffic light; **into**—make the *t* into an arrow; **all the**—put hands on each *l*, reaching out; **world**—draw faces looking through the *w*; **and preach**—make the *p* or *h* into someone talking; **the good**—draw happy faces in each *o*; **news**—make the *w* into arms holding a newspaper; **to all**—make the *o* very big and place "all" inside it; **creation**—make some of the letters (*t,i,o*) into people.)

Students display completed words. Read verse together.

Verse Hunt Clues

Materials Checklist

- ☐ large sheet of poster board
- ☐ small index cards
- ☐ felt pen
- ☐ scissors
- ☐ pencil

Preparation

Letter Bible memory verse on a large sheet of poster board. Cut verse into as many jigsaw pieces as you expect students in the group (see sketch). Hide all puzzle pieces around the room. Letter a clue on an index card for each puzzle piece, describing where puzzle piece is hidden.

Procedure

As students arrive give each one a clue card, then say, **There is a secret message in this room. To discover the message use your clue card to find your puzzle piece. When everyone has found a puzzle piece we will assemble the message.** After students have completed the puzzle, read the Bible memory verse.

This is how God showed his love among us: He sent his one and only Son into the world that we might live through him. 1 John 4: 9

Verse Orchestration

Materials Checklist

☐ chalkboard and chalk

Preparation

Letter words of Bible memory verse on chalkboard.

Procedure

Recite the Bible memory verse several times with students. Divide class into two teams. One team will recite portions of the Bible verse. The other team will illustrate each portion with an action. Direct teams to perform parts as shown in example below.

After practicing several times, allow teams to switch parts.

Team A: "If I speak."

Team B: (Moving hands like a mouth.) **"Yak, yak, yak."**

Team A: "But have not love."

Team B: (Hanging head and moving it from side to side.) **"No love."**

Team A: "I am only a resounding gong."

Team B: (As if hitting a gong.) **"Bong! Bong!"**

Team A: "Or a clanging cymbal."

Team B: (As if hitting cymbals together.) **"Crash! Crash!"**

Quick Quote

Materials Checklist

- ☐ Bible
- ☐ small index cards
- ☐ felt pens
- ☐ chalkboard and chalk or newsprint
- ☐ dictionary

Preparation

Letter the Bible memory verse on chalkboard or newsprint.

Procedure

Divide group into pairs. Give each pair of students index cards and a felt pen. Students letter words to verse, two words on each card. Have students add the Bible reference to last card. Pairs then work together to memorize verse. Erase the verse from chalkboard. Have pairs shuffle their cards. When teacher says "go," pairs race to put cards back in the correct order. If time allows, remove several cards from each set and have pairs try to put them in order again. Ask, **What does this verse tell us about God?**

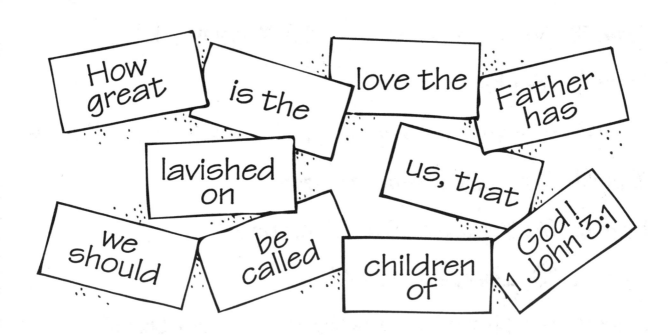

Clothespin Verse Pass

Materials Checklist

For each student—

- ☐ clothespin
- ☐ slip of paper

Preparation

On slip of paper letter the words to the Bible memory verse, three or four words on each paper. (There should be one slip of paper for each team member.) Make a set for each team of four or five students.

Procedure

Divide group into teams of no more than four or five members each. Give a clothespin to each student. Teams line up and players stand at arm's length. Teacher places one set of verse slips on the floor near the feet of the first person on each team. All the phrases should be visible but not in order. When teacher says "go," the first player on each team uses his or her clothespin to pick up the first phrase of the verse. He or she then passes the slip to the second player, who takes it with clothespin and continues passing it. When last player receives the phrase, he or she places it on the floor and runs to the front of the line to pick up the next phrase of the verse. That player beings passing the phrase down the line. Repeat procedure until one team has successfully passed the entire verse to the end of the line, put it in order and said it aloud together.

Verse Tangle

Materials Checklist

- [ ] large ball of yarn or string
- [ ] chalkboard and chalk

Preparation

Letter Bible memory verse on chalkboard.

Procedure

Students sit in chairs or on the floor in a circle. Read Bible memory verse several times with students. Hand ball of yarn to one student. Instruct him or her to hold the ball of yarn in one hand and to hold the loose end of the yarn with the other. That student then throws the ball of yarn across the circle to another student while saying the fist word of the verse (and while still holding the loose end of yarn). The player who catches the ball says the next word while holding the yarn strand and throwing the ball to another student. Continue until verse has been completed several times.

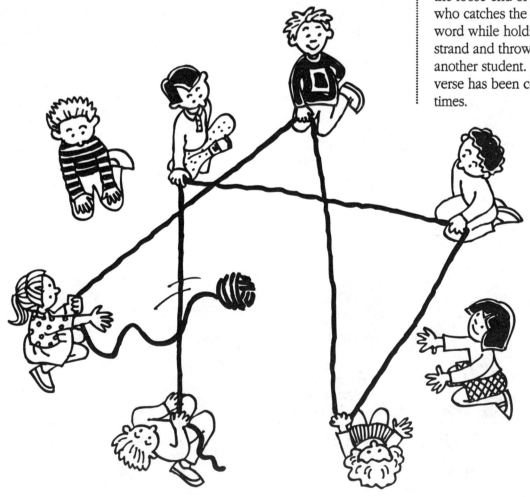

Modern Art Gallery

Materials Checklist

- [ ] two large pads of paper and two felt pens or chalkboard and chalk
- [ ] paper and pen
- [ ] masking tape

Preparation

On sheet of writing paper write at least 10 questions relating to the life application of the lesson. (Example: "What is a way to show that you honor your mom?")

Procedure

Divide class into two teams and have each team sit on floor. Leader stands in front near paper or chalkboard. Teams each choose an "artist" to draw. Leader reads aloud Life Application question from paper. Artists then silently write their answers on the leader's paper, visible only to leader. At leader's signal, the artists quickly draw pictures of their answers, without speaking or drawing letters or words. Teams try to guess their artist's answer. The first team to guess the correct answer gets one point and play continues with a new pair of artists. When all answers have been drawn, the team with the most points wins. Display art pictures in assembly area.

Billboard Contest

Materials Checklist
☐ large sheets of poster board
☐ felt pens

Preparation
None.

Procedure
Divide class into groups of three to four students. Give each group a sheet of poster board and several felt pens. Each group designs a billboard with a slogan that communicates the message of the day (see sketch). Set a time limit for groups to complete billboards. Each group presents their billboard to the class to be judged by applause. Billboard with the loudest applause wins the contest. Display billboards in assembly area.

STOP RUNNING AND START RESOLVING

Junior/Life Application

Fruit Mix-Up

Materials Checklist

- [ ] poster board
- [ ] felt pen
- [ ] one slip of paper for each child
- [ ] pen
- [ ] tape or tacks

Preparation

Letter the fruit of the Spirit on poster board. Use tape or tacks to attach poster to wall.

Procedure

Review with children each fruit of the Spirit. Each child secretly letters one of the five fruit of the Spirit on a piece of paper. Say, **To play this game you need to be prepared to pantomime a way you can show each of the first five fruits of the Spirit in your life. For example, what are some ways you can show love to another person? How can you show that you have joy? Peace? When can you be patient? Kind?** Lead children in suggesting a variety of answers. At your signal, players silently mingle and try to find other players with the same fruit of the Spirit. Players may not say anything, but must act out their fruit of the Spirit. For instance, if a child's paper reads "kindness," he or she might walk around patting other players on the back. For "love," player might hold his or her hands over heart. When player find someone with a matching paper, they stick together, pantomiming their word, until they find the rest of their group. Game is over when all groups have formed. Repeat game as time allows by redistributing slips of paper.

Junior/Life Application

Search and Assemble

Materials Checklist
- [ ] large index cards
- [ ] felt pens

Preparation
On index cards, write two or three statements summarizing the Bible story and its application to our lives—a short phrase on each card (see sketch). Make an identical set for each group of three or four students. Hide cards around room or outside area.

Procedure
Divide class into teams of three or four students. Teams search for hidden cards and attempt to piece together each statement. (Each team should have two or three complete statements.) Students may trade unneeded duplicate cards for needed cards from other teams. The first team to complete statements and read them aloud together is the winner.

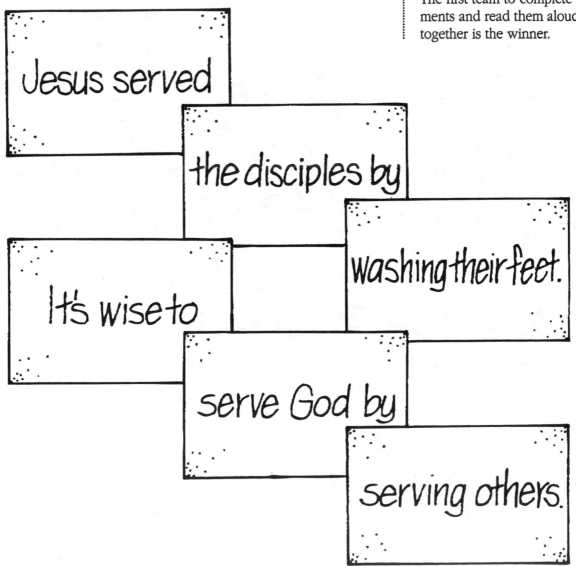

Team Acrostic

Materials Checklist

- ☐ graph paper
- ☐ rulers
- ☐ pencils

Preparation

On each sheet of graph paper, outline a grid with at least 20 vertical columns. (*Optional:* If class time is limited, number the students' grids in advance, following the instructions.)

Procedure

Divide the group into teams of two or three students each. Give each team a sheet of graph paper and a pencil. Instruct them to locate the center column on the page and write a 0 (zero) at the top. At the top of the first column to the right of the center, they write 5 (five), 10 (ten) at the top of the next, then 15 (fifteen), 20, 25, 30, etc., out to the end of the grid. At the top of the first column to the left of the center, they write 1 (one), then 2, 3, 4, 5, etc., out to the end of the grid. Have each team write a key word (Example: promise, generous, encourage, etc.) from your lesson in the center column.

Instruct the teams to write on their grid words which are important in the lesson, either from the story or the Bible memory verse. Each word must use one of the letters from the word in Column Zero. Every letter counts points, so longer words are more valuable than short ones. Also, more points are scored for letters to the right of Column Zero than for those to the left, thus it is better to think of words which begin with the letters in Column Zero than words which end with those letters. Students are allowed one "free" word which does not have to be related to the day's lesson. A team should use its "free" word for a letter where they are stumped. After allotted time is up, teams total their scores. (Example in sketch is worth 472 points.)

9	8	7	6	5	4	3	2	1	0	5	10	15	20	25	30	35	40	45	50
									P	R	A	Y	E	R					
	R	E	S	U	R	R	E	C	T	I	O	N							
									O	L	I	V	E	S					
									M	O	U	N	T						
I	N	T	E	R	N	A	T	I	O	N	A	L							
			A	L	W	A	Y	S	(S)										
					A	N	G	E	L	S									

Solutions

Materials Checklist

- [ ] index cards
- [ ] blank sheets of paper
- [ ] pencils
- [ ] envelope

a.

Solutions

Jill	Devon
Park	Church
Money	Greeting Card

b.

People	Places	Objects
Carla	Home	Greeting Card
Erin	Mall	Clothing
Michael	School Cafeteria	Food
Devon	Park	Bicycle
JR	Schoolbus	Books
Jill	Church	Money

Preparation

None.

Procedure

Divide class into teams of two to four players. Give each team six index cards and a pencil. Each team works together to list two of each of the following (one on each card): names of people in the group; places a person might obey God; objects a person might use when obeying God (sketch a). When students have finished writing, combine all the cards in each category. Read each card aloud and have a member of each team write on a sheet of paper all the items you read. This will be the team's clue list (sketch b).

Next, secretly draw one card from each category and place them in the envelope. Teams will be competing to guess which three cards are in the envelope. Combine all remaining cards, shuffle and pass out an equal number to each group. Each team looks at the cards they are holding and crosses these items off their clue list since they know these items will not be in the envelope. Play begins as a member of Team A attempts to guess which cards are in the envelope by saying something like, "We think *J.R.* obeyed God in the *cafeteria* by sharing his *food*." Team B then shows Team A one of the cards they are holding that will prove their guess is incorrect, such as a card saying "food." Team A crosses the word "food" off their clue list. Team B then guesses and Team C shows a card. If the team next to the guessing team can't prove them wrong, they say, "We can't help you." The next team must then show a card which will prove the guesser is incorrect. If no team can prove the guesser wrong, then the guesser has correctly named three cards in the envelope. The first team to guess correctly wins.

Person, Place, Thing Skits

Materials Checklist

- [ ] three shoe boxes
- [ ] slips of paper
- [ ] pencil
- [ ] felt pen
- [ ] variety of items such as: baby rattle, plastic flower, box of raisins, note card, bag of cookies, wallet, keys, sponge

Preparation

Label each box with a different word: "Person," "Place" or "Thing." Letter each slip of paper with a different person, such as: "mom," "dad," "teenage boy," "teenage girl," "12-year-old boy," "12-year-old girl," "baby," "grandma," "grandpa," "teacher." (Make a "person" slip for each student.) Place these slips in the box labeled "Person." Letter slips of paper with a variety of places, such as: "home," "school," "store," "hospital," "restaurant," "park," "bus." Place these slips in the box labeled "Place." Place items listed in materials section in box labeled "Thing."

Procedure

Divide group into teams of three students each. Each student draws a slip of paper from the "Person" box. Then each team draws one slip of paper from the box labeled "Place" and one item from the box labeled "Thing." Groups have five minutes to plan a skit based on the information and item chosen. The skit should illustrate a way to show love. Each group performs a skit for class.

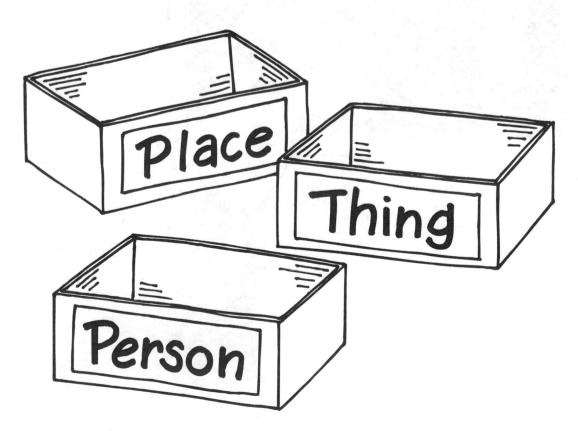

203

Draw 'n Guess

Materials Checklist

☐ chalkboard and chalk

☐ paper and pencils

☐ watch with second hand

Preparation

None.

Procedure

Divide group into two teams. Team members work together to brainstorm ways to show God's love, and write each idea on a slip of paper. Then a member of the opposite team selects one of these slips of paper, goes up to the chalkboard and quickly tries to illustrate the way to show God's love while his or her team guesses. Teams take turns drawing and guessing until each idea has been drawn. Teacher times each draw 'n' guess sequence and records each team's time. The team with the lowest time at the end of the game wins.

Two-Bag Skits

Materials Checklist

- [ ] two large brown grocery bags
- [ ] various items to use as props (clock, car keys, football, wallet, telephone, etc.)
- [ ] five slips of paper
- [ ] pen

Preparation

Choose several Bible verses students have recently memorized. Letter a different verse on each slip of paper. Place slips of paper in one paper bag. Fill the other bag with at least ten items to use as props.

Procedure

In pairs, students come forward and draw two props and one slip of paper from the bags. Pair then uses the props to perform an impromptu skit illustrating a life application of their verse. (Example: Pair draws wallet, clock and verse about forgiveness. One student looks nervously at clock, awaiting 5 o'clock when "dad" will be home. Other student plays the dad who arrives home and takes out his wallet, wondering why his money is gone. Son confesses to taking money and asks for forgiveness.) After each skit, the group tries to guess which verse was being illustrated.

Bag It!

Materials Checklist

- [ ] paper bag
- [ ] several items from the list below (see *Procedure*)

Preparation

Place the items in the paper bag.

Procedure

Students take turns removing items from the bag, one at a time. Say, **In what way could you use this object (wisely, to show kindness, to obey God, to praise God, etc.).** Volunteers tell as many responses as possible. *Items and responses could include:*

Pen—write a letter to someone.

Dollar—give money to help someone in need.

Picture book—read to a younger child.

Wrapping paper—give a gift to someone.

Dish cloth—do the dishes without being asked.

Fork or spoon—set or clear the table.

Bible—read God's Word or share a verse with a friend

Food package—give food to the hungry.

Note card—write a thank-you to someone who has done something special for you.

Adhesive bandage—help someone who is hurt.

Cross necklace—tell others about Jesus.

Eyeglasses—look for ways to help others.

Family photo—thank God for those who love you.

Trash bag—help keep your church or home clean.

Index

Index